The Secret Erotic Paintings

Pictures and Descriptions of Classical Erotic Paintings, Bronzes and Statues

By

Colonel Fanin

Translated from the French by

Famin, Stanislas Marie Cesar

First published in 1871

Published by Left of Brain Books

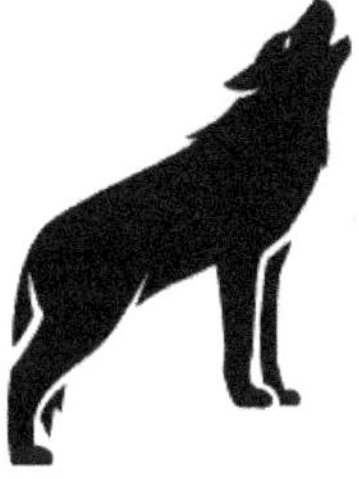

ISBN 978-1-396-32680-6

First Edition

PUBLISHER'S PREFACE

About the Book

"The ancient Roman and Greek cultures had a very different attitude about sexuality than successive European cultures, more akin to that of the Kama Sutra. This, of course, was unimaginable to latter day Europeans, who rigidly compartmentalized body, mind and spirit, and to whom any sexuality was sinful and morbid.

Some of the best artistic expressions of this can be found in the recovered city of Pompeii. Pompeii was frozen in time by the volcanic eruption of Vesuvius in 79 A.D., and not unearthed until 1748. Pompeii was a seaside resort, devoted to the arts, relaxation, and the pursuit of pleasure. The excavators were horrified to discover erotic frescos, mosaics, statuary and phallic votive objects. The moveable erotic artifacts were taken to Naples and kept in seclusion in the Royal Museum. The erotic wall and floor art had lockable metal boxes constructed over them and were displayed to tourists for an extra fee (women and children excluded). When I visited Pompeii in the late 1960s, this peepshow was still in operation.

This work is a translation of a book by a 19th Century French antiquarian Cesar Famin. In 1816 (according to a citation in the Library of Congress catalog) he published (under the initials M. C. F.) Musee royal de Naples; peintures, bronzes et statues Erotiques du cabinet secret, avec leur explication containing sixty lithographs of the best erotic artifacts in the Naples collection. The name of the artist is unknown. The volume was published with the cooperation of the Naples museum in a very limited edition. The French authorities confiscated and destroyed most known copies of the original book. One ended up in the 'Private Case' of the British Museum. There is also a copy in the Special Collections of the Library of Congress.

In 1871, an English translation of Famin's work was published in England under the byline of 'Colonel Fanin'. Privately printed in a limited edition, this translation became one of the rarest erotic books. [...]

Famin's text to accompany the images is deeply conflicted. He is obviously drawn to the subject matter and has a deep understanding of the significance of the artifacts. He also takes every opportunity to condemn Classical sexual practices and cultural values. Whether this is a figleaf or a sincere reaction is impossible to determine. However, in spite of the 'shocked, shocked' attitude in Famin's text, it contains quite a bit of valid and well-researched information, including quotes from classical authors and details of mythology, artistic methods, spiritual practices, architecture, and literature.

These pictures are fairly explicit and aren't for everyone. Few of the items on display here are excessively purient by contemporary standards. These are historical cultural artifacts, not pornography. Nonetheless, consider yourself warned."

(Quote from sacred-texts.com)

CONTENTS

INTRODUCTION

THE pious Emperor Theodosius abstained from destroying the not very decent statues and other relics of the heathen, in order to perpetuate and expose all the absurdity and infamy of false religions, and to inspire contempt and hatred of them."--Sylvain Mareschal.

THE recollection of the past is the delight and the consolation of old age. In all times the generation about to die out has declaimed against the morals of the rising generation. This concordance of opinion having been transmitted from century to century, it might be expected that as we go back towards the epoch of the Creation we should, come to a golden age of virtue and purity. By the same reasoning, we should as we pass on in fancy to the series of centuries to come, reach an epoch of such depravity that the mind might well refuse to conceive all its enormity. But let us reassure ourselves: this is only the sport of an uneasy imagination, a weakness incidental to humanity. Civilization, far from corrupting manners, tends rather to mollify them. While there was yet in the world but one man and one woman, there existed between them a partnership in guilt. While there were yet only three men, there was already a hoary perjurer, a fratricide, and an innocent victim.

The Holy Scriptures, as well as the profane histories of the first and greatest peoples of the world, present nothing but a series of revolting atrocities. Nimrod founds slavery: entire populations given up to the most shameless debauchery perish by fire from heaven, and the lake Asphaltites swallows up in its poisoned waters the foul remnants of Sodom and Gomorrha; Lot lies with his own daughters; a king of Jerusalem has the feet and hands of seventy princes and nobles cut off, and makes them crawl under his table; Abimelech ascends the throne, borne on the corpses of his brothers whom he has assassinated; Aristobulus condemns his mother to die of hunger; Herod orders the children under two years of age to be massacred. Let us draw the curtain on the bloody and shameful pictures which the histories of Greece and Rome display: they have been sufficiently described.

2

"Are you inclined to fancy that our race is for ever deteriorating? beware of the illusion and the paradoxes of the misanthropist. Man, discontented with the present, imagines a deceitful perfection in the past, which is only the mask of his own discontent. He extols the dead out of hatred to the living; he beats the children with the bones of their fathers.

"To prove the existence of this pretended retrograde perfection, you must ignore the testimony of facts and reason; and if there remains a doubt about past facts, you must ignore the unchanging fact of man's organization; you must prove that he is born with an enlightened perception of the use of his senses; that he can without experience distinguish poison from food; that the child is wiser than the old man, the blind man surer in his step than the clear-sighted; that the civilized man is more unhappy than the cannibal; in a word, that there no longer exists a progressive ladder of experience and instruction," &c.--Volney: Les Ruines, chap. xiii.

Evil and ignorance were born with the world itself, and God willed that man should in course of time grow better as he grew more enlightened. He left him the task of perfecting His work as soon as he knew all its beauty. Knowledge and virtue will reign on the surface of the globe; but, alas! their power, when it has reached the culminating point, will descend again to the cradle; and the end of a great period will be signalised by a reawakening of evil and ignorance. Such is the immutable law: everything is born to die; everything dies to be born again!

It is the office of a voice more eloquent than ours to proclaim these great truths. We who are only obscure lovers of science are contented to examine certain relics and traditions appertaining to the epochs of antiquity, and we say with sincere conviction that manners are now sweeter and purer than they were then; that, in a word, we have with greater knowledge acquired greater virtue.

We are not unaware that certain blind partisans of ancient times pretend that the obscene nudities which continually appear in the literature and art of the palmy period of Greece and Rome, are only indications of simplicity and candour. The savage tribes even of our own day may serve, they say, as a further support to this hypothesis. But what should we thus have to admit? That modesty is only hypocrisy; that the ancients whose language and customs were impregnated with such obscenity, were better men than we who throw a thick veil of mystery over our most innocent weaknesses.

You talk to us of savage tribes; but consult those travellers who are most worthy of belief, and they will all tell you that there exists in them an innate feeling of modesty which civilization rapidly develops. And is the rude islander better than the civilized man because he is less modest? Is it also from his simplicity and candour that he attaches such value to staining his tomahawk with the blood of his fellow-man; that he makes a hideous cup of his skull, and finds so much pleasure in a feast of human flesh?

Or did Petronius when he sang a shameful victory over a young stripling; Virgil when he sighed for the beautiful Alexis; Ovid and Horace when they celebrated incest and adultery in pompous verse; deserve to obtain civic crowns together with the poetic palm?

Before Christianity had revealed to the world its great civilizing secrets, men rendered a strange worship to those material objects which acted most directly on their senses. It may even be supposed that a very long time before the Christian era there was no other worship than that of symbols. The divinity who presided over the reproduction of the human species, the miracle of all epochs, deserved the purest homage. That vague desire which precedes the union of two lovers, the burning pleasure which marks its accomplishment, the soft languor that follows, all received a name, a soul, an attribute, and Love was hailed as king of heaven by the acclamation of the world:

Not safely shall we seem Love's lightest law:
He reigns, and holds the highest gods in awe.--Ovid. Epist. iv.

A worship born with the first feeling of love was above all consecrated to the emblem of virility. Even to this day the Arabs call it to witness when they desire to make a solemn oath: and the peasants of Apulia call it "the holy member (il membro santo)." It was raised into a divinity who presided alternately over marriage, pregnancy, country pastimes, the preservation of fruits, streams, fountains, and groves.

The water woos the soft green grass,
And the green grass attracts the lover.--Desmoustiers.

Legislators felt the necessity of consecrating a worship which singularly favoured the development of population, and they consequently themselves set the example of fanatic devotion to a religion which they inwardly despised.

If Diodorus, Plutarch, Pausanias, Origen, Saint Jerome, Ruffinus, and several other writers both ancient and modern, may be credited, the worship rendered to the phallus, or Priapic emblem, connects itself with the history of Osiris. Here in a few words is what is related on this point:--

Osiris, an Egyptian prince, the husband of Isis, went off to a distant war, leaving to his brother Typhon the charge of governing his kingdom during his absence. The latter cruelly betrayed the confidence of his brother; he sought to seize the throne and to corrupt his sister-in-law. Osiris on his return endeavoured to conciliate his brother by gentleness and forbearance; but the traitor, hiding his perfidy under the mask of hypocrisy, conceived the horrible project of putting an end to his rival's life. With this object he invited him to a great feast at which several officers of his court, who were devoted to him, were present. After the repast a large chest was brought in, and Typhon proposed to each guest to try if he could enter it, and fill up the inside. He tried it himself first; and when his brother's turn came, the conspirators threw themselves above him and shut him in. The chest containing the royal victim was thrown into the Nile.

Isis, in despair at the death of her husband, walked along the banks of the river in the hope of finding there his precious remains. At last she learnt that they were in Phœnicia, hidden under reeds: she proceeded thither without delay, found the object of her ardent search, and carried them back to Egypt. But the implacable Typhon, being informed of this circumstance, had his brother's body taken away, and cut into several pieces which were dispersed in diverse directions. The unfortunate Isis collected them with care, procured them to be buried, and consecrated the genital parts which she had not been able to find: at her death, which happened a short time after this event, the Egyptians placed both her and her husband in the rank of the gods. Festivals and mysteries were instituted in their honour. The representation of the phallus of Osiris, consecrated by Isis, was home in public processions, and the worship of this emblem of conjugal love soon became general in Egypt. Herodotus speaks of a famous feast among the Egyptians and Greeks, which he designates by the name of Φαλλαγώγια or

Περιφαλλέα, 'the feast of the phallus, (II. 48, 49,) [1] and adds that women suspended to their neck little figures representing the organ of virility. Osiris became, in the mind of the people, the symbol of the sun, the principle of fire, the generator of all nature, and it is remarkable, in fact, that all ancient religions have agreed on the same doctrine, only differing in the liturgy by which they expressed it. The Scythian, the Egyptian, the Phoenician, the Persian, the Babylonian, the Indian, the Greek, the Etruscan, and the Roman, were all agreed on this point. The famous worship of Mithra is no other than that of the Sun, of Osiris, of the lingam, of fecundating virtue. It is the same with that of Bacchus, of Apollo, of Vesta, &c. It is not unknown also that the Zend-Avesta is the book of a similar religion, as its name "living fire," indicates. In short this same worship has followed the long roads of civilization, and arrived even to us. In several of the departments of France the custom still exists of lighting great fires on the eve of St. John's Day, the period when the sun is at its highest; that is to say, the summer solstice. The same custom existed not so very long ago at Paris: in Dulaure's history it may be seen that the kings of France accounted it a duty to be present on these occasions. And in order that nothing may be wanting to complete the resemblance, the custom of certain towns in France, and notably of the South, is to intersperse the bonfires of the feast of St. John with besprinklings of cold water, which the common people liberally bestow on each other, amidst laughter and noisy demonstrations of joy. Who can fail to see here a disfigured remnant of the sacerdotal and the mystic ablutions of antiquity?

The Phoenicians, in adopting the worship of Osiris, transmitted it to the Eastern populations. The phallus was worshipped by the Moabites and Midianites under the name of Belphegor. In effect, Baal, a divinity often mentioned in the Holy Scriptures, and to whose name the Moabites added the name of Phegor, signifies with this addition naked god, an attribute agreeing with that of Priapus. According to what we read in the Book of Numbers, fornication was consecrated to Belphegor; and--to sum up all-- the Vulgate translates the name of Mipheletzeth, which is the same thing, by that of Priapus (Vossius De Idol,, lib. II. cap. 7). The Phrygians took from the Moabites the worship of this strange divinity, and it received among them, particularly at Lampsacus, the greatest development. This people worshipped the idol under the name of Priapus, whom they supposed to be

---

[1] The priests charged with carrying the phallus were called phallophores; and this was a dignity much sought after.

a son of Venus and of Bacchus, and they instituted feasts and mysteries in his honour. From them ultimately the worship was transmitted to the Greeks, as we learn in Herodotus, and from the Greeks it passed on to the Romans. St. Augustine declares that in several towns of Italy, not only was the phallus borne in triumph in public processions, but that obscene songs were sung in its honour; and in fine, that it was solemnly crowned by the gravest of the matrons (St. Augustine, City of God).

Among these peoples the exhibition of the phallus or lingam in the temples was originally a consequence of the mutilation of certain priests who, that they might the better honour their Divinity, denied themselves those pleasures which seemed made only for Him: but later, the priests retained the symbol, and abstained from mutilation.

The mysteries to which this religion gave rise are known under many names we will mention the most famous of them:--

Dionysia, or Dionysiac festivals, in honour of Dionysus, the Bacchus of the Greeks, so called from Dios, the genitive of Zeus (Jupiter), the father of Bacchus, and from Nusa, his birthplace.

Bacchanalia, of Egyptian origin, which differed little from the Dionysia. In the latter a pig and in the former a he-goat was sacrificed.

Lupercalia, derived from lupus, because the dog, another emblem of the phallus, is the enemy of the wolf [1].

Brauronia, licentious mysteries.

Homophagia, in which the jugglers who ate raw meat played a part.

Orgies, from the word orge (ὀργή), rage, anger.

Thyes, from Thya, the mistress of Bacchus, whence the Bacchantes have been called Thyades.

---

[1] There was in Egypt a country named Lycopolis, where wolves were worshipped. Tradition, according to Diodorus, said that Isis and Horus, her son, preparing to give battle to Typhon, Osiris returned from Hades in the shape of a wolf, and aided them in their enterprise. Might not this be the real origin of the Lupercalia?

Pyrodulia, the worship of fire.

Orphic feasts, orgies of Bacchus, instituted by Orpheus.

Orneas, Priapeas, festivals of Priapus.

Cotyttia, festivals in honour of Cotytto, the goddess of debauchery.

It remains for us to add that superstition, born of the excesses of a burning imagination in southern climates, attributed extraordinary virtues to the priapic sign. Women who were barren suspended little phalluses in bronze or stone to their necks; men followed by maleficent genii also carried it about them to keep off sorceries; pilgrimages were performed to the temples of Priapus; the knee was bent in worship before the phallus; at a certain period of the year the virginity of a young girl was sacrificed to the god. On these occasions the victim was placed on the virile attribute of the statue of the god, and there remained during the entire accomplishment of this shameful and cruel homage. "The newly married woman was wont to be placed on the upright instrument, which was fixed in her privy parts, in order that the god might seem to have the first outpouring of her virginity" (Lactantius).

Lactantius here speaks of the god Mutinus, who had a temple at Rome; but it may be safely inferred from a passage in St. Augustine that this divinity was no other than Priapus himself (City of God, vi.)

At last Christianity came and sapped the foundations of this abominable worship. The idols were overturned; but men kept the recollection of them at the bottom of their hearts; and, with pain it must be said that, while, varying the forms of these impure rites, they have perpetuated the usage of them. Thus in Italy, where superstition has struck deep roots, the attribute of virility is considered a sure safeguard against evil spirits. In Naples especially, and in Sicily, every one carries about them (women on their bosoms, and men on their watch-chains) little horns of coral, lava, ivory, &c. Some of immense size may be seen in the antechambers of persons one would never have suspected of such a weakness, and no one blushes to admit that they are talismans against witchcraft. Modesty has substituted these for the phallus of the ancients, to which also were attributed preservative virtues against witchcraft. Indeed we may see several of these obscene presentations furnished with a quantity of little bells; it cannot therefore be doubted that these objects were used as amulets, seeing that bells were consecrated to Priapus, who was also called The Noisy (Βριήπυος). Theocritus said that the noise of bronze chased away impurities (ἀπελασικὸν τῶν μιασμάτων). May it not be a traditional remnant of this superstition that makes the country people believe that the noise of the bells keeps away storms?

Nothing is more curious to observe than the veneration of certain modern populations for these ornaments considered as talismans. In Italy, when a man happens to have neglected to take with him one of these singular amulets, it is not unusual to see him place his hand affectedly on his genital parts, at the sight of any person whose untoward features awaken suspicions of evil hap. Further than this we have ourselves many times seen credulous men in Sicily, and women too, testify the greatest possible respect to a priest or monk, by lightly touching his virile parts with the tip of their fingers, and afterwards devoutly kissing their own hands. In Spain it is the same; and among the Mahometans pregnant women hold it as a great consolation to be able to kiss the sexual parts of a madman. In the East the worship of the phallus has been perpetuated with still greater unreserve; and the lingam or pulleiar worshipped amongst the Indians, is, as is well known, a symbol of the union of the two sexes.

Another tradition, resting on testimony too doubtful to deserve serious examination, has caused some writers to say that the worship of the phallus had its origin at Athens, after the cessation of a venereal epidemic. In sign of joy and gratitude, processions took place, of which the gravest matrons formed part, bearing on their necks representations of the genital parts of their husbands restored to health. Whatever we may think as to the truth of this tradition, it is unquestionable that these obscene images were for a long time an ornament much in request among ladies. Portraits of women have been brought to light, otherwise very decently clad with necklaces composed of a series of little phalluses; voluntary exvotos to which another image of the god was added by the lady as often as he heard her prayer. In the same manner the daughter of Augustus put as many garlands every morning on the image of Priapus as she had offered sacrifices to him during the night.

Let not the reader deceive himself as to the expressions 'grave matrons' and 'respectable ladies,' which we borrow from writers of the middle ages!

The customs to which the women of antiquity devoted themselves, were dissolute and scandalous; the nudities of that epoch, and the impure writings of its authors, are unchallengeable witnesses to the libertinism which then prevailed in all classes. It was a time when men did not blush to make known to the world that they had obtained the favours of a fair youth, and when women honoured themselves with the name of Tribades. These latter were themselves living memories of the fabulous hermaphrodites, on the subject of whom we must now enter into some details.

A son of Mercury and Venus, endowed with rare beauty, stopped one day near a fountain whose pure and tranquil water invited him to bathe. The Naias Salmacis became so smitten with this beautiful youth, that she offered him her most secret favours; but finding him either too timid or too insensible, she died of grief The gods took pity on the unhappy woman, raised her to life again and united her with her lover by confounding their sexes, "so that they can neither be said to be woman or boy; and seem both neither and either." [1]

This singular being, at the same time man and woman, was called hermaphrodite, from Hermes, the Greek name of Mercury, and Aphrodite, the surname of Venus born of the sea-foam. Did not fable intend to designate by this allegory those women who, born under a burning climate, seek after every kind of pleasure with both the sexes? Some few, favoured or rather afflicted by nature with an extraordinary conformation, which physiology understands and explains, are in a condition to obtain for their accomplices an ephemeral enjoyment without end or object, and consequently without excuse. It is moreover an attested fact, that real hermaphrodism exists not, and cannot exist except in the Vegetable kingdom, and among a few imperfect animals, such as molluscs and zoophytes; but never among perfect animals, especially mammiferous ones.

The Greeks gave also to the hermaphrodites the name of Androgynes, a word which explains itself. It is not extraordinary that populations, given up by education and temperament to all the excesses of amorous passions, should have accorded the honours of deification to individuals whom they considered as the most happily organised; since they could at the same time give and receive pleasure. Resisting the one in order to prolong the charm of an amorous struggle, attacking the other with the fire and daring

---

[1] OVID.

of an inflamed lover, the hermaphrodites seemed created solely to love and to enjoy all. They were generally represented with a woman's breast, which confirms our opinion that such beings had no real type among the ancients, except in individuals of the female sex whose conformation presented a deformity. They held a leaf of water-lily in their hands: this plant was consecrated to them, because it floats on the surface of limpid waters, and has the quality, it is said, of calming amorous desires, circumstances which recall the history of Salmacis.

The Satyrs and Fauns were considered at the same epoch as rural duties, at the head of whom was placed the god Pan, or Priapus, whom mythologists often confound: they were represented with the figure and bust of a strong and hairy man, and with the horns, tail, and feet of a goat. It was said that these maleficent divinities dwelt in the woods, where they were the terror of the shepherdesses. We need only suppose the satyrs to be nomadic shepherds, such as still exist in Sicily. These rude and barbarous men were clad in goat skins; and living constantly in the midst of rural solitudes, the sight of a woman excited their amorous desire do the highest point, and they passed entire days occupied in watching for their prey. When the favourable moment came, they flung themselves impetuously upon the victim, and by force and threats obtained an imperfect pleasure. The terror which these pretended divinities inspired was such that sacrifices were everywhere offered to them, and the statue of their chief, Pan or Priapus, was placed as a scarecrow on the border of estates to keep off robbers and intruders. On these occasions the god was represented with the bust of a man, and the lower part of the body ended in quadrangular stone. He was then called Hermes, and he was confounded with Mercury, the god of thieves. But what is most remarkable is that the statue generally bore a gigantic phallus, an object of fear and respect.

Pliny, the Naturalist, thinks that the Satyrs were nothing but great apes; yet their existence was for a very long time believed in; and grave men still credited it in the Middle Ages. Regarding this, a curious work of Conrad Lycosthenes, entitled "A Chronicle of Prodigies and Wonders," may be consulted. The following is what he writes on the subject of Satyrs; we give a literal translation:--

"Satyrs. Quadrupeds living in the mountains of the East Indies, endowed with extreme swiftness, with a human face and the feet of a goat, having the body covered all over with hair, having nothing of human character, but delighting in sombre forests and fleeing the society of men. The ancients worshipped these monsters as rural divinities, saying that Fauns, Sylvans, and Satyrs were the forest-gods. The Pans presided over the fields, and the Sylvans over the woods, although poets have confounded them. Saint Jerome thus expresses himself on this subject: 'I have seen,' he says, 'a little man with a hooked nose, whose forehead was furnished with horns, and the lower part of whose body ended in feet like those of a goat.' Having then made the sign of the cross, Saint Jerome asked him who he was, and he is said to have replied to him: 'I am a mortal, one of the inhabitants of this solitude, whom ignorant paganism, in its vulgar error, calls Satyrs, incubi, &c.'"

We also find in the "Historia Monstrorum" of Aldrovandus, the following passage:--

"Several authors rightly place Satyrs, Tritons, Nymphs, Nereids, and Sirens, tinder the nomenclature of men of the woods. It is here proper to speak of each of these beings. As for the Satyrs, so called from the word σάθη, which signifies the virile member, because they are always disposed to libertinism, we adopt as most reasonable the opinion of antiquity. Pliny assures us in several parts of his writings that there exists in the equatorial mountains of India, a country called Cartadules, where live the Satyrs, a species of horned men, hairy, very agile, having the human face, feet like a goat's, with nothing of the character of man, delighting themselves in the obscure recesses of forests; their velocity is such that they can only be taken when they are old or ill. Pomponius Mela adds that these men are half savage and have nothing human except the face; and he says elsewhere it has often happened that fires have been seen to glow during the night in the mountains of Mauritania, beyond Atlas, and that the noise of cymbals and pipes has been heard whilst in the daytime nothing was discovered there; whence it follows positively that they are Faun and Satyrs."

Such are the absurdities which were repeated in the sixteenth century!

Here all important question presents itself. Were these supernatural beings who appear to us in the night of ages as a strange phantasmagoria, created by the fruitful imagination of the sages of antiquity to serve as symbols of the laws which sway the intellectual world? Should we see in the hermaphrodite only an ingenious hieroglyph indicating the necessary and absolute union of the sexes in entire nature and in the god Pan, with the bust of a man and the feet of a he-goat, only the great All, the universe, a wonderful aggregation of beings of every kind? or indeed is not this interpretation given to fable itself only a reasoning by induction, a philosophical explanation of those conceptions which, false as they were in their consequences, were true in their principle? We are inclined to hold the latter opinion. In short, we do not think there were first found poet-philosophers who conceived the Pans, the Satyrs, the Venuses, the hermaphrodites, as pure symbols, and that afterwards their disciples personified these chimerical conceptions by applying the names and attributes of the divinities to shepherds, apes, courtezans, and exceptionally-organised women. Such a feeling appears to us absurd, since to adopt it we must admit that science has pre-existed; that the world had no infancy; that civilization was not the result of a kind of progressive groping in the dark. It seems to us much more natural to suppose that the earliest societies, composed as they were of beings ignorant, inquisitive, and fear-stricken, were led to deify the creatures, from whom by divers means, they received impressions of joy or grief, delight or terror, and to suppose in them qualities they did not really possess. In all ages the marvellous has held the greatest empire over our mind. At a later period, enlightenment spread among men: the wisest among them felt the impossibility of maintaining a worship based on ignorance; but the time was not yet come for proclaiming the truths which it was reserved for Christianity to unveil, and for several centuries they were compelled to content themselves with allegorical explanations which were given to vulgar errors into which the earliest forms of society had fallen. When it is said that Bacchus and Osiris are only personified emblems of the sun, it must not be supposed that these divinities were always symbolic. There existed in the beginning of societies beneficent men, and illustrious chiefs, who were the primitive type of Bacchus, Jupiter, Hercules, and several other gods of paganism, whom it is very easy to distinguish from those who are purely symbolical. It was not till long afterwards that more enlightened men made of them emblems of pure imagination, and it must be admitted that nothing is so easy as to symbolize thus all the phenomena of nature by the aid of men of genius and talent, or by help of their most remarkable actions. Nor does this imply any contradiction of the motives we suppose to have guided the chisel or pencil of the artists of antiquity: we may clearly see with our own eyes that in seizing upon the foolish ideas of his predecessors, the statuary who caused a beautiful hermaphrodite or ardent Satyr to start forth from a formless block, had no other object than to exercise his talent in the reproduction of all kinds of beauty. Tatian has bequeathed us a catalogue of painters and statuaries who had represented the celebrated women of their epoch under emblems of divinities. Tatian, Πρὸς Ἕλληνες, pp. 168, s. 99. Arnobius, Clement of Alexandria, and Pliny declare that artists took pleasure in making Venuses and Satyrs, solely to give scope to their capricious imagination, and to flatter the unruly passions of their contemporaries. Arnobius, Adv. Gent. vi., Clement of Alex. Προτρεπτ., p. 35. Pliny, xxxv. 110.

Therefore, to sum up in a few words the solution of this question, we think that in the beginning of societies, men believed at first in the real existence of their gods, and that only long afterwards they began to consider them as symbols.

The Greeks had the pride to give a national origin to their divinities, and yet they could not be ignorant that they had become acquainted with them through the Phoenician or Egyptian colonists. It may be remarked further, that other peoples whose origin dates back to far antiquity, such as the Etruscans, had the same symbols and the same groundwork of religious ideas as the Greeks. Only a few years ago there were discovered in certain localities of ancient Etruria, at Cornetol, Canino, Chiusi, Cortone, and other places, some antiquities of purely Etruscan origin, necropolises, numerous hypogea, and also vases and paintings where the principal subjects of Hellenic mythology may be seen represented.

As soon as the imagination of poets had invaded the domain of divinity, it created a mythology. The gods were classed in several orders, and the most powerful among them, Love and Venus, presided over the pleasures of the senses and over physical enjoyment. Jupiter merited the first place in the palace of the gods, because he was considered as the most powerful athlete in amorous combats. It was by similar exploits likewise that Hercules merited his apotheosis. The noisy troop of divinities of the lowest order also presided over carnal pleasures, or seemed created solely to use them with excess. Pan, endowed with the lustfulness of a he-goat, was represented with the horns and feet of that animal. The god Faunus approached nearer to humanity; he differed from man only by a hairy excrescence resembling a tail, by his pointed ears, and sometimes by two little horns partially concealed under his hair.

The Satyrs were the companions and in some sort the subjects of Pan; the Fauns obeyed the god from whom they derived their name.

Redoubtable divinities had been created in honour of women: it became necessary to imagine some that should satisfy the passions of men. The fields and woods were peopled with creatures equally beautiful and passionate, with lovely and voluptuous nymphs. Daughters of Ocean, they made the plants fruitful. Arnongst them the Oreads presided over the mountains, the Dryads over the forests, the Hamadryads over trees, with which they were united without power to detach them selves, the Naiads over rivers, and the Nereids over the sea-waves.

This pompous retinue of the most lascivious divinities was well calculated to exercise the ardent genius of the poets of Egypt, Greece, and Rome. Aided by the multitude of ambitious, of greedy, or of sensual men, they placed the mythological worship on broader bases; they instituted feasts, mysteries, and processions of every kind. They celebrated games in honour of Jupiter, the lord of thunder, father of the sun, the principle of fire which fertilises the universe; mysteries under invocation of Isis and Osiris of whom we have already spoken; Bacchanalia in commemoration of Bacchus, the conqueror of India, a god who also presided over generation, and who some learned men declare to be the same as Pan, Jupiter, and Osiris; and lastly solemnities consecrated to the generative principle.

In the Ithyphallic feasts consecrated to Bacchus, the priests called Ithyphalli or Ithyphallophores, carried in evidence of their office an enormous virile member, of red leather, attached to their haunches with straps.

We have already spoken of the phallophores.

All these infamies flattered man's senses; but they became more and more intolerable as civilization assumed a higher development. The religion of materialism was at last annihilated before a religion of spirituality; morality was revealed to the earth, and the idols of the temple were shivered at the church-porch.

Notwithstanding this, several of those relics in which science takes so lively an interest, have survived the lapse of centuries. They have been preserved in the womb of the earth to transmit to future generations the lessons of history. Those which we have chosen to form the subject of this book were discovered in some of those towns situated on the side of Vesuvius, which had been buried under its volcanic ashes. We allude to Herculaneum, Pompeii, and Stabia.

There exists a multitude of works written in all the languages of Europe in which interesting details have been given of the towns just named. It therefore appears to us superfluous to repeat here what has already been said so often, and notably by Mazois, in his great work on Pompeii; by Sylvain Mareschal, in his explanation of the paintings of Herculaneum; and by the learned Canon Jorio, in several of his writings. It will suffice us to recal to mind that these towns of Greek origin, the foundation of which dates back to fabulous epochs, and which became subject to the Roman dominion about three hundred years B.C., were buried under the eruptions of Vesuvius in the year 63 of the Christian Era according to some authors, and 65 according to several others, under the reign of Nero; it seems, also, that the city of Herculaneum survived those of Pompeii and Stabia for several years, and was not swallowed up till the year 79, under the reign of Titus Vespasian. Every one knows that the elder Pliny died at Stabia, suffocated by the volcanic smoke, a victim of his love for science. The memory of this event has been transmitted to us in a letter of Pliny the younger.

During more than sixteen hundred years even the site of the destroyed cities was unknown; learned men were still at controversy on the subject at the beginning of the eighteenth century, when chance led to the discovery in a country-seat of the Duke of Lorraine, at Portici, of a fruitful mine of objects of art and antiquities of all kinds. The King of the Two Sicilies caused excavations to be made, and in the month of December 1738 the theatre of Herculaneum was found. The excavations made at this period, and continued down to our own days, have furnished the Neapolitan government with the richest, most instructive, and most interesting collection of antiquities. However, Herculaneum, which had not been swallowed up by a torrent of lava, as Sylvain Mareschal and other writers have erroneously maintained, but which had been buried under a shower of those little pumice-stones which the Neapolitans call grapillio, and of which whole mountains are found in the neighbourhood of Naples, was not destined to come forth from its tomb: in order to dig out this city entirely it would have been necessary to destroy the towns of Portici and Resina. It was thought sufficient to make explorations by means of subterranean caves which were filled up again from time to time. So that, with the exception of the theatre, to which you descend by a species of well and survey by the glimmer of torches, and of a few houses discovered and dug out only a few years ago, a visit to Herculaneum offers but little interest; and it is the same with Stabia.

At last, a few years after the discovery of Herculaneum, a peasant digging the ground at a mile's distance from the town called Torre d'Annunziata, and six miles from Naples, broke with his spade the capital of a column. He carried the fragments to Naples, and Pompeii was discovered.

The operations which have been successively carried on by order of Charles III., Ferdinand I., Joachim Murat, Francis I., and which are daily being continued, have led to the excavation of about a fourth part of the city. An enclosure of walls irregularly surrounded the town, which might contain from thirty to forty thousand inhabitants. You reach it through the village of Augustus the Happy (Pagus Augusti felicis). This is the consular way, lined with magnificent tombs. In this village we find a house of which the proprietor was a freedman of Augustus, named Arius Diomedes. We will give further on a few details respecting the architecture of this house. After having surveyed the dwelling (illegible--JBH)owed of its masters, and read with emotion the touching inscriptions graven eighteen centuries ago through maternal tenderness and filial piety, we enter Pompeii. The rays of a burning sun once more penetrate into those streets which the earth had concealed in its recesses during a long series of centuries. We survey with unspeakable emotion that Roman city, whose inhabitants, we might suppose, have temporarily gone away to escape from a contagion. Does an open door present itself to you? Make haste and enter the house before its owner returns from the fields! What would he say if he saw you imperti-nently directing your steps into the interior of his apartments, if he perceived that you had collected together the household utensils which the negligence of his slaves had forgotten, into the comer of the house? Would you know the name the master of this abode? Read it on his door as you enter; it is written there in red ink; read also that of the neighbours, you will soon know the whole quarter: "Albinus, Modestus, Pansa, Salustius, &c.

It is a subject of no little astonishment to see in this town, which otherwise was inconsiderable, this immense quantity of temples, columns, and monuments of every kind, irrefragable witnesses of that love of the arts carried among the ancients to so high a degree. We visit successively, and not far apart from each other, a vast amphitheatre capable of holding eight thousand spectators, the basilica, a magnificent palace devoted to purposes of justice; the temples of Venus, Mercury, Isis, and Jupiter, the Pantheon, and others.

These buildings belong to the Grecian style of architecture; and the Doric order may be remarked there throughout, giving to these imposing ruins an air of solemnity which commands respect. What a multitude of sensations begin to crowd on the traveller who casts his curious eye over such noble remains! He wanders alone through the streets, the markets, the public places, where once a numerous population thronged and stirred on every side to satisfy its passions, interests, and wants . . . A mournful silence now reigns in all the thoroughfares of the deserted city; everything in it bears the impress of profound sadness; we should say in a word that the walls plunged for so long a time in the night of the tomb, can no longer bear the light of day.

The Neapolitan government [1] has reserved to itself the exclusive right of causing excavations to be made in the precincts of Pompeii; but by going through some formalities, an authorization may be obtained to make researches at Nola, in Apulia, in the Basilicata, and other provinces. The minister of the king's household then solely exercises the right of becoming first buyer; that is to say, of purchasing any objects which may suit him, at a valuation fixed by a commission consisting of the Director and three conservators of the Museum.

The architecture of the private houses, being very nearly uniform, we intend to describe one of these dwellings in order to give an idea of all the others: we choose that of Arius Diomedes, in the village of Augustus the happy.

The house has two stories, of which one is above and the other below the level of the street; in the middle is a sufficiently large square court, around which is a straight peristyle (impluvium) sustained by brick columns coated with stucco. Under this peristyle we perceive a series of rooms placed one after the other, without communication between them. These rooms are small and not very commodious, like all those in the town. In fact we know that the ancients lived much out of doors, in the middle of the court we see two large cisterns in which rain-water was kept.

____

[1] The original was published in 1857.

The first apartment to the right is a reception-saloon called exedra, after which comes a gallery called basilica.

To the left are apartments consisting of bath-rooms, or nymphæa. They are five in number, each one being devoted to a special purpose: in the first, nymphæum, the bath-water was made hot; in the second, apodyterium, the bather relieved himself of his clothes; in the third, balneum, was the bath; the fourth, unctorium, contained perfumes and essences for rubbing the skin after leaving the bath, and the fifth and last was used for vapour baths.

By the side of these nymphæa, or saloons, are found the bedrooms, cubicula, three in number.

The lower story comprises the festal saloons, the triclinium and cænaculum, and the cellars where may still be seen vessels called dolia, for keeping liquors.

The house, like all the others, is built of brick; the rooms are paved with little stones of about half an inch square, of diverse colours, and artistically grouped in mosaic. The walls are covered with stucco and with paintings which, according to the destination of the rooms, represent fruits, flowers, animals, and mythological subjects.

Among the well-to-do persons there was a retreat consecrated solely to the worship of Venus; the Greeks called it Aphrodision and the Latins, Venereum. It was preceded by a sort of antechamber (procæton) where the cubicular slave lodged His employment was to watch over the safety of this chapel of love; he drove away intruders; and he kept in a casket the shoes, which were an object of great luxury with the Roman ladies, and which they often laid aside during the day, even before sitting down to table: the slave bringing them when wanted out of the casket in which he had placed them. Plautus calls these servants Sandaligerulæ and Menander Sandalothekas.

The cubicular slave was also entrusted with the bringing of the water and the perfumes for ablutions.

It is in places like these that erotic paintings have been discovered.

The use of obscene representations was frequent in antiquity. There were few houses without some of those lascivious paintings which the Greeks called grylli and the Latins libidines. [1] Two painters, Polignotes and Parrhasius, are often referred to by Pausanias and Pliny as having excelled in this kind of composition. [2]

Several paintings on marble have been discovered; but those which form the subject of this book are frescoes which decorated the walls of houses in Pompeii and Herculaneum.

Vitruvius has made known with some detail the methods used in this kind of painting; and as the explanations given on this subject by M. Mazois leave nothing to be desired, I shall, confine myself to relating succinctly that these methods consisted in covering the partition of the wall requiring to be painted with several coatings of a kind of mortar made of lime and pozzolani. When the last coat of plastering was perfectly dry, a finer paste called opus albarium or opus marmoratum was passed over it. This was what we call stucco. Then the painter's task began. (Vitruvius, Book 7, chap. 3.)

The ancients had two ways of mixing colours; diluting them in some water with gum and glue, or mixing them with melted wax. The latter method produced the colours called encaustic. Paintings were called monochromes or polychromes according as they were produced with one or with several colours. Cinnabar was generally used in monochromes. It often prevails in polychromes. These frescoes are for the most part of very mediocre quality; but we must remember with Pliny that the most skilful artists of antiquity did not amuse themselves by painting on walls; this task was confided to painters of the lowest class. PLINY. VITRUVIUS, ubi suprà. The drawing is often incorrect, and always hard and dry. The laws of perspective are ill observed, and the medley of colours is as strange and capricious as it is fatiguing to the eye.

Independently of the rooms called venerea in private houses, there were, in the Roman towns, places of debauchery called lupanaria. MARTIAL, Epig.

---

[1] Grylli, from γρύλλος, a pig. The etymology of libidines requires no explanation.
[2] PLINY, xxxv. 7, 10; xxxvi. 5. PROPERT. Eleg. II. &C., MARTIAL, EPIG. xii. SUETON. xliii. 2. 12 & 13. PAUSANIAS, Description of Greece.

I. 35; xi. 46. TERENCE'S Comedies. Several of these have been discovered at Pompeii. Over the entrance-door of one of these may be seen a large Priapic sign in stone; in others, lascivious paintings have been discovered. And to conclude, in a quantity of private houses, both at Pompeii, at Stabia and at Herculaneum, erotic subjects have been found, sculptures in bronze, marble, rock-crystal, terra cotta, et cetera;--phalluses, Bacchic amulets and other obscenities.

These objects have been deposited in a private cabinet of the Royal Museum at Naples. Admission, forbidden to women and children, is only granted to men of mature age by means of special permission from the minister of the king's household. This collection is the richest of its kind; but there also exist Florence, Dresden, London, and Madrid, private galleries where obscene relics, brought from Egypt, Greece, and Etruria are kept.

Independently of the objects of which we give copies and explanations, the secret cabinet of the Museum of Naples possesses several cupboards in which a large quantity of phalluses in bronze, bone, ivory, or isinglass, of various dimensions, have been placed. We considered it superfluous to reproduce all of them; this long and difficult labour would have been without interest, after giving and explaining those which appeared to us to deserve the preference.

From the study and comparison of these antiquities, the mere inspection of which gives alarm to our modesty, results the fact that before the Christian era there was no other creed than that which might be called the theophallic. The universe, that marvellous assemblage of beauty of every order, would soon have ceased to exist without that generating principle perpetuated in animals and plants, and everywhere vivifying, inert matter. If a man impregnated his consort, he thought he had created; and when it happened to him to carry his thoughts back to a first man, he supposed that two divine beings, supernatural, pre-existent, and of different sex, had carnally united to create the human race. The first sons of the gods inherited a wider share of the paternal power; of which they availed to metamorphose themselves into animals of every kind, according as pleasure called them to the bosom of the waters, to the plains of the air, or the entrails of the earth. Thence arose the origin and worship of animals.

It was thus that a voluptuous mythology established itself on earth, and modified a thousand times by place and circumstance, perpetuated itself during a long series of centuries.

We need not regret the departure of those times when modesty had no cloak when, like the brute, man and woman stood before each other, unabashed at their nakedness. The facility of enjoyment gave birth to satiety and disgust. A frightful corruption of morals was the inevitable consequence of this state of things, for excess of debauchery could alone reanimate desire, the prime mover of enjoyment.

Eternal glory to the religion which overturning these impure idols into the mire, and unrolling the code of chastity before our eyes, has made our sensations purer and our pleasures keener. Thanks to it, the end of existence has ceased to be a disgrace, and the principle of all that is has shewn itself in its purity.

THE SATYR AND THE GOAT

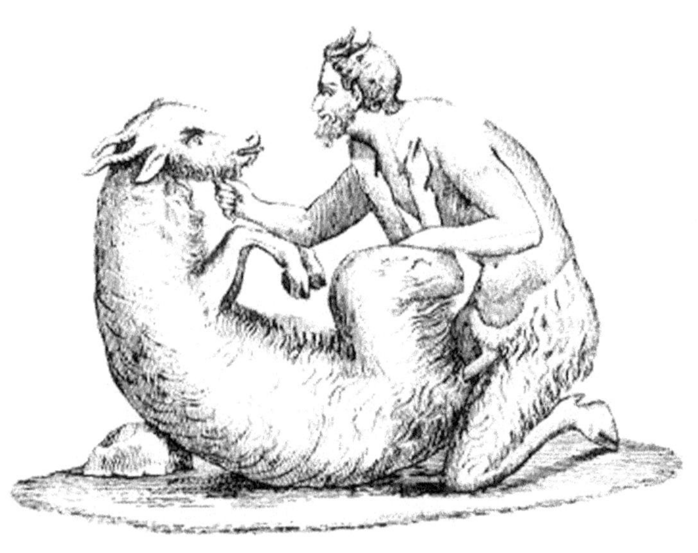

Plate I.

THIS group, found among the excavations at Herculaneum, is more remarkable for the expression which gives life to the marble than for the purity of the execution. It might especially be wished that the goat were more correctly drawn; but it is impossible not to admire the expression of sensuous passion and intense enjoyment depicted on the Satyr's features, and even on the countenance of the strange object of his passion.

The crime of bestiality was not rare among the ancients, and it was not confined to the intercourse of men with female animals; it extended also to that of women with males. Herodotus (Book 2, § 46) informs us that in his time a surprising thing happened in Egypt, in the Mendesian nome, a he-goat had intercourse publicly with a woman, and the fact was widely and generally known. But it is true the Egyptians might be inclined to excuse this crime, being, as they were, under the conviction that the god Pan frequently metamorphosed himself into a he-goat. In their language the god and the animal were both alike named Mendes.

In our own days there still exist, in Sicily and Calabria, half-savage herdsmen who pass whole days in profound solitude, and come for a few moments only every evening into the villages, where bread and oil are distributed among them. These men, whose sole task is to watch over the preservation of flocks, often conceive an insensate passion for the animals confided to their care. The same thing also happened to the shepherds of Virgil's time:--

"We know that towards thee in the obscure nook
The jealous he-goats cast an angry look,
While in the shade the nymphs with laughter shook;"

Virg. Eglog. III.

Plutarch says:--

"When Nature, supported though she be by law, cannot contain your intemperance within the bounds of reason, as if it were a torrent carrying it away perforce, she often and in many places commits great outrages, disorders, and scandals against nature in the matter of the pleasure of love; for there have been men who have conceived a passion for goats, sows, mares, &c." [1]

---

[1] PLUTARCH. Discourse on the Reason of Beasts, xvii.

MARSYAS AND OLYMPUS

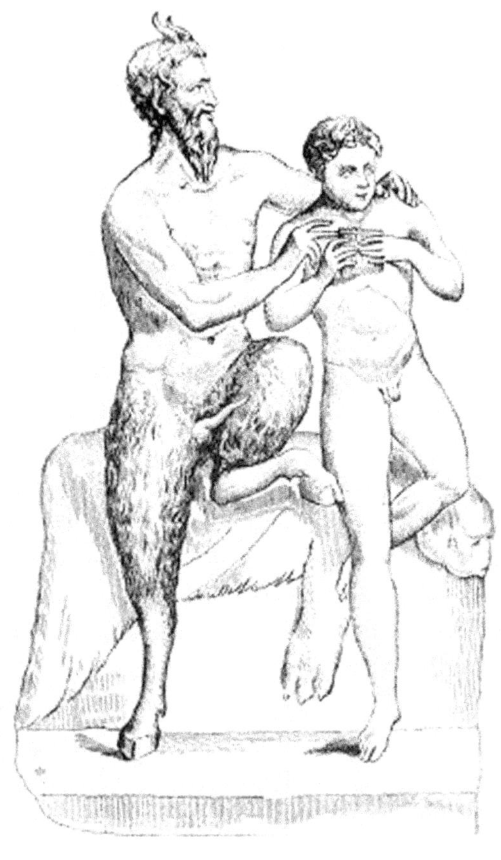

Plate II.

MARSYAS, the Satyr, the inventor, according to several mythologists, of the pastoral flute, is represented in this group, one of the masterpieces of antiquity, at the instant when, while giving lessons on that instrument to young Olympus, he is preparing to attack the chastity of his pupil. His feature, on which a god-like majesty is impressed, betray the transports of his passion, to which he appears to wish to abandon himself: his mouth and nostrils open to fan the fire of concupiscence which devours his breast. His left hand rests on the youth's shoulder, as if to draw him towards him, and one of his legs, which he lifts up in order the better to secure him, leaves no doubt as to the object of his desires. The youth, meanwhile, looks down, confused and abashed; he seems to break off his music; and we fancy we see him tremble in every limb.

A rock, on which a lion's skin is spread, serves as a seat for the Satyr.

Olympus, a son of Meon, a native of Mysia, lived before the Siege of Troy. Plutarch attributes to him the composition of several hymns in honour of the gods. Ancient authors agree in representing him as a pupil of Marsyas, whom Pliny has confounded with Pan Suidas speaks as follows

"Olympus (a son of Meon, a Mysian), a flute-player and poet, a disciple and favourite of Marsyas. He lived before the Trojan war, and gave his name to Mount Olympus in Mysia."

This subject has been several times treated by the artists of antiquity. Among others a painting was found at Herculaneum which has none of the obscenity of the group here described: Marsyas is there represented with the features of a Faun and the legs of a man. [1]

According to Pliny, the invention of the pastoral flute, composed of several reeds bound together, and called fistula or syrinx, is due to Pan. [2]

The above group is taken from the Farnese Museum.

---

[1] Pausanias, x. 30.
[2] Pliny, vii. 56.

VENUS CALLIPYGE

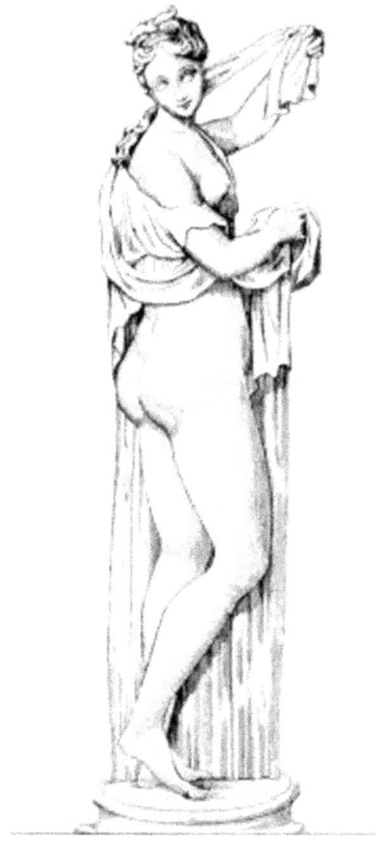

Plate III.

THIS Charming statuette, found at Rome, was placed in the Farnese palace, and thus came into the possession of the King of Naples, together with the ownership of that edifice. It does not form a portion of the cabinet of private works of art, but is placed in a reserved hall, where the curious are only introduced under the surveillance of a guardian, though even this precaution has not prevented the rounded forms which won for the goddess the name of Callipyge, from being covered with a dark tint, which betrays the profane kisses that fanatic admirers have every day impressed there. We ourselves knew a young German tourist smitten with a mad passion for this voluptuous marble; and the commisseration his state of mind inspired set aside all idea of ridicule.

It is impossible, indeed, to imagine anything more graceful than the Venus here spoken of. The power of beauty is recognized wherever it manifests itself: the marble seems to palpitate; in contemplating it modesty takes alarm, desire begins to awake, and imagination to kindle; and we are obliged to hurry away in order to restore our agitated senses to their original tranquillity.

The goddess is raising the light tunic in which she is enveloped; her beautiful head is turned backwards, and her look, which glances lightly at a wonderful bend of her loins, seems to arrest itself with gratification on those graceful contours for the sake of which altars were erected to her.

Athenæus relates as follows the origin of the worship of this Venus:--

"In those far-distant centuries mankind were so given over to the pleasures of the senses that they built a temple to Venus Callipyge. This was how it happened. A countryman had two fair daughters; they were contending one day with each other about the beauty of their hips, each declaring that hers were the most beautiful, and so disputing they came upon the highway. A young man happening to pass that way whose father was already well in years, they at once submitted themselves to the judgment of his eyes, and he pronounced in favour of the eldest. But at the same time he fell so deeply in love with her, that he had hardly arrived at the town before he fell ill, kept his bed, and told his young brother what had happened to him. The latter hastened to the fields to look at the young girls, and fell in love with the youngest. Their father sought in vain to persuade them to unite themselves with better families. So, being obliged to yield, he obtained the consent of the father of the two sisters, whom he sent for immediately from the fields, and married his sons with them. This event caused the name of Callipyge to be given to the two wives among their fellow-citizens, as Cercidas of Megalopolis relates in his iambics.

"These two women, having thus become rich, they caused a temple to be erected to Venus, whom they named Callipyge, according to what Archelaus tells us in his iambics." (Deipnospohistes.)

The worship of Venus Callipyge was extensively spread over. the whole Greece, where it was still preserved for a long time after the fall of other divinities. It passed over to the continent of Italy, where it did not find fewer devotees, and where it served in some sort as an encouragement to a passion equally outrageous and criminal. The Venus Callipyge was powerless to destroy the abominable worship of the Hylases and Antinouses, and it became itself a new element of debauchery in the shameless times of the Roman decline. It was not then unusual to see scenic games in which young girls appeared entirely naked; the public judged between them in certain contests of the same nature as that which sprang up between the two sisters of whom Athenæus speaks, and the empire received the news as an event.

The voluptuous figure which forms the subject of this article derives its erotic charm chiefly from the arrangement of the vestments. It may in fact, be remarked that absolute nudity is less immodest than partial or accidental nudity. When the Spartans in the circus, and the Romans at the theatre, saw young and beautiful girls entirely naked, they certainly experienced less voluptuous sensations than when they happened accidentally to catch sight of the nakedness of a woman who might fall awkwardly from her horse, or slip on the pavement of the street. Complete nudity argues a state of independence and freedom which possesses nothing alarming to modesty or seductive to the senses; but partial nudity seems as if reserved for furtive and unusual actions. In order to feel this fully, one should see side by side the Venus de Médici, a chaste divinity entirely nude; and the Venus Callipyge, a voluptuous courtezan, indecently clad.

Numerous copies have been made of this statue. A very remarkable one exists in the park of Versailles.

SARCOPHAGUS

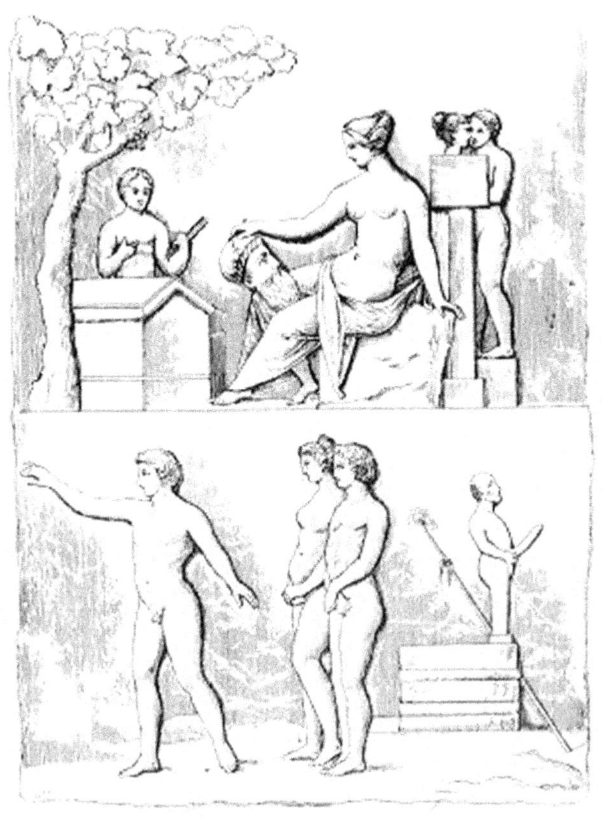

Plate IV.

WE are shown by this bas-relief the two principal sides of a sarcophagus, where, without doubt, a married pair were buried: the sculptor has reproduced their features, together with the most important epoch of their life. The first side represents the two, glowing with youth and beauty, at the solemn moment of initiation. They are naked, according to custom, as is also the hierophant; but the latter is free in his movements: he is no longer ashamed of his nudity, for nature lies underneath him, he has knowledge of sacred things, and he reveals them to the young supplicants. But the latter appear abashed and surprised; they listen devoutly to the sacred words of the hierophant, and keep their hands crossed over the place where modesty would require a covering.

In the background we perceive a Priapus-Hermes, a little bald old man, who holds in his hands a large phallus. The wine-vat, which serves him for a pedestal, and the thyrsus, which rests by his side, sufficiently indicate the Dionysiac mysteries, so called from Bacchus, who was surnamed Dionysus: we shall speak of these more at length in the explanation of Plate VII.

The second side presents a symbolic representation of the ceremonies practised at funerals. A woman is seated on a rock near a tomb. Her head-dress, a kind of turban, indicates mourning; for among the peoples of antiquity, as among the Hebrews in modern times, the custom was to veil oneself and to cover one's head in token of respect or grief: the contrary is the case among Christians. This woman carries in her hands a tragic mask: these masks were likewise employed at the theatre, at festivals, in war, at triumphal solemnities, Bacchanalia, and at funerals.

Near the figure, a kind of post, probably bearing an inscription, indicates the limit of life at which the faithful married pair, whose memory it is desired to honour, met again, after having descended the stream of life together. To the right we perceive a tomb: it is placed under an oak. This tree was properly that of Jupiter, of his mother Rhea, and of Pan; but the Goddess Hecate, the Diana of Hades, also crowned herself with oak-leaves. The shepherds of Arcadia were called acorn-caters, and claimed to be descended from an oak-tree.

Behind the tomb, a youth, whose bust only is seen, holds in his hands a broken wand, an image of the existence just extinguished. He appears to be speaking, and is doubtless pronouncing an eulogium on the defunct couple.

THE GOD PAN ON A MULE

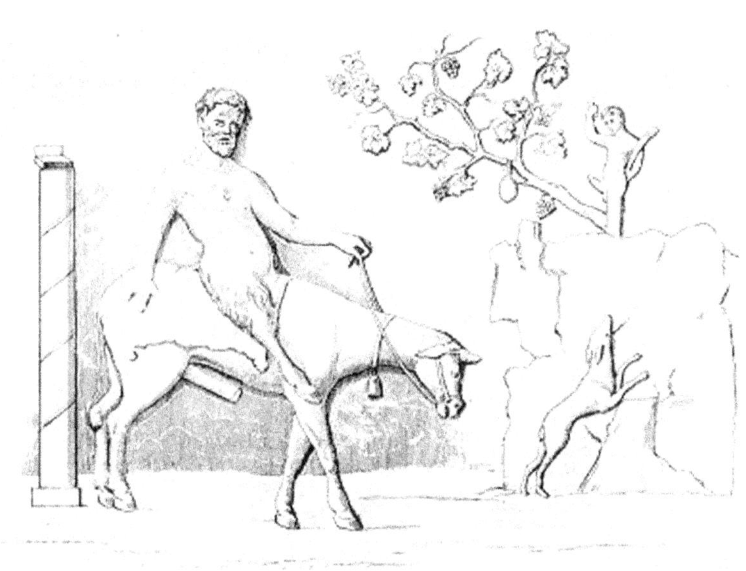

Plate V.

IN this bas-relief the god Pan is mounted on a mule, of which the covering is made of a leopard's skin. A little bell is suspended to the animal's neck, which proves this custom, still kept up in Italy and Spain, to be of great antiquity. In Sicily, where the mule is an indispensable beast to the traveller, it carries a necklace of little bells, whence a most wearisome tinkling proceeds; but he will seek in vain to purchase from the muleteer an exemption from this disagreeable accompaniment. Whether from prejudice, or from positive experience on their part, they declare that, if deprived of their orchestra, the mules would sleep on their way, and might fall over the precipices with which the roads are not unfrequently bordered.

On this bas-relief the animal seems to be neighing, and he even accompanies, with an expressive gesture, an action which among beasts of burden indicates an amorous sensation. The position of his legs sufficiently indicates that he wishes to stop: but his rider makes every effort to compel him to pursue his road; he leans backward, strikes him on the crupper, and raises the bridle. The face of the god is full of expression; his lower lip is protruded to make way for the exclamation well-known to all muleteers: dgia. But who can thus retard the progress of the mule which bears so noble a burden? One would say that he recoils before the statue of Priapus, which is perceived on a mass of rocks to the spectator's right. This Hermes, stripped of his usual attributes, holds in his hands two objects which it is not very easy to distinguish: one is, perhaps, a little cup, the other a cornucopia, or horn of plenty, or simply a club. The ancients were sufficiently inclined to represent the divinities who presided over the reproduction of the human species with the horn of plenty; and this symbol of fecundity is an application so easily understood, that it would be useless to explain it here. Generally, among the fruits with which this horn was filled, might be seen the quince, a fruit consecrated to erotic enjoyment. Among the Romans a quince was given to a newly-married pair to cat before conducting them to the nuptial bed.

The Priapus-Hermes of this bas-relief rises, as we said, over a mass of rocks. Doubtless he is the guardian of a garden, placed on the limit of the estate, with the inscription, which the dimensions of this fragment do not admit of our distinguishing. On an antique marble referred to by Grutler,[1] from Boissard, may be seen a Priapus between two baskets of fruit and flowers; a club lies by his side; and we read on it also this inscription: To Priapus Ithyphallus, club bearer, keeper of gardens and chastiser of thieves.

An oak extends its vigorous branches over the Hermes: this tree was consecrated to Priapus, to Pan, and to all the rural divinities. To one of the branches is suspended a cymbal, the offering of a devout Bacchante, and at the foot of the tree may be seen a little altar, surrounded by a sort of garland. Against the rocks stands a dog, and appears on the point of springing upon the Hermes.

---

[1] GRUTLER, Pl. xcv.

Behind the god Pan we observe a Doric column. It supports a small open casket: this is the arca ineffabilis, in which the image of Bacchus was shut up at the Dionysiac mysteries, or Bacchanalia.

Pan, who here plays the chief part, is represented, as usual, with pointed ears and goat's legs. According to the principal mythologists, he was the son of Penelope and Mercury: this god desiring, as they say, to triumph over the chastity of the wife of Ulysses, metamorphosed himself into a he-goat, and by this means obtained what he desired; the god of the Satyrs was born of this union. This is, it must be admitted, a pleasant way of preserving to Penelope her reputation of chastity! Weighing the two faults together, she had better have yielded to a young and beautiful god than to a filthy beast. According to another version, no less shocking and absurd, Penelope, far from showing herself so severe as has been supposed with respect to her admirers, granted, on the contrary, her favours to all of them, and Pan, which signifies all in the Greek language, was the result of the intrigue.

Setting aside these ridiculous interpretations, we will remind the reader in this place of a fact of which we said a few words in the introduction to this work. The first idea of Pans, Satyrs, and Fauns originated in the mind of the men of ancient times in consequence of their positive ignorance, their prejudices and superstition, and not as the result of a high and eminently mystical conception. Then, as now, shepherds who passed long months of the year in profound solitudes, sometimes conceived a criminal passion for the animals entrusted to their care. The crime of bestiality is still in our own day frequent enough among Sicilian herdsmen. Among women it has always been rarer, but not unknown. The ignorance of the men of this epoch made them think that from these unions arose extraordinary beings, half men and half goats. These same herdsmen often committed outrages which rendered them objects of fear, and consequently of respect. If it happened that one of them offered violence to a young girl in the solitudes of the valley, the parents of the victim did not fail, whether from interest or credulity, to make it known that their daughter had been seduced by one of those rural divinities who partake both of the man and the brute. Hence arose the worship of pans and satyrs; hence the origin of the nymphs, the dryads, and hamadryads. It is needless to add that legislators and priests laid hold of these ideas and used them to govern the multitude. And our learned men do far too much honour to antiquity when they would fain see mystic conceptions, ingenious fictions, and brilliant allegories where nothing existed but materialism and ignorance.

INVOCATION TO PRIAPUS

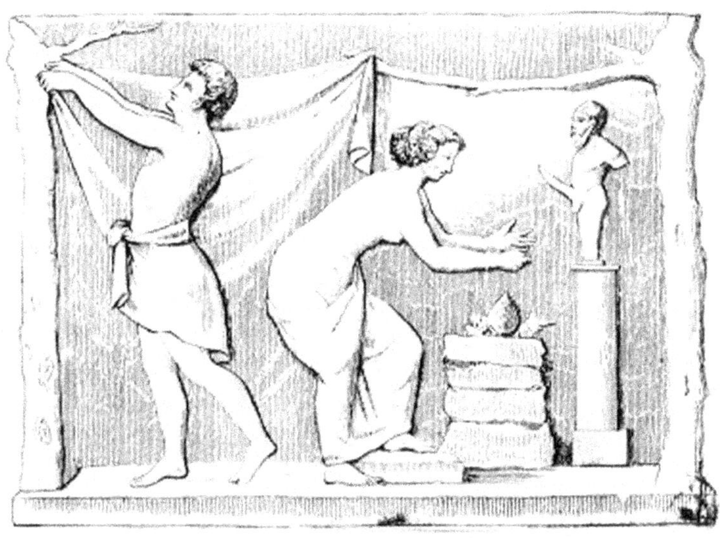

Plate VI.

EVERYTHING in this bas-relief indicates an interior scene, an act of candour and piety, and not a disgusting orgy. The a married pair, clad as decently as the nature of the sacrifice to which they are about to proceed will allow, seem to be asking the god who presides over generation to put an end to a grievous sterility; the expressive gestures of the woman, especially, bear out this explanation. The husband is occupied in stretching out a curtain which is to veil from profane eyes the mysteries of the sacrifice.

Procul esto, profane!

The god, represented with the figure of a bald-headed and bearded old man, reposes on a little column, before which we observe a kind of altar erected in haste by the married pair, on which they have placed some oak-leaves and the pine-apple which surmounted the thyrsus of the priestesses of Bacchus.

The execution of this piece is not without some merit. The figures in it are expressive and harmoniously grouped; but the defects are sufficiently obvious to enable us to dispense with enumerating them all. It will easily be perceived, for instance, that the man's back shows too much convexity; that his legs are too short and his arms too powerful. Doubtless nature is often thus made, but not that which artists use as a model.

BACCHANALIA

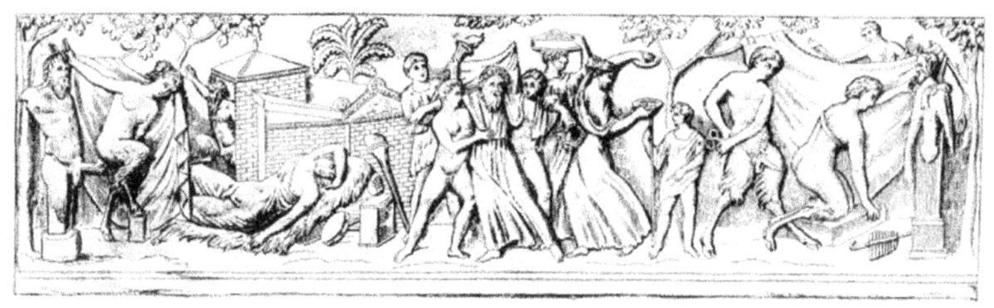

Plate VII.

ONE of the most celebrated pagan festivals, known by the name of Bacchanalia--and sometimes disguised with slight modifications, under the appellations of Eleusinia, Dionysia, Lampteria mysteries of Isis, of the Cabeiri, of Mithra, Adonis, the Bona Dea, &c.--is represented in this curious bas-relief. All these mysteries, and the greater part of those which we have omitted, had also their dogmatic, liturgic, and moral side; they differed not so much in doctrine and moral tendency as in origin and rites. The generating power symbolised, a victim sacrificed and purifications of the faithful,--these pervade all.

The Cabeiri, gods deriving their name from the Arabic word Cabir (power), were four in number--Ceres, Persephone, Pluto, and Mercury. With the initiated Ceres was called Oxieres; Persephone, Axiokersa; Pluto, Axiokersos; and Mercury, Casmilus. Many of the celebrated men of antiquity, such as Moses, Orpheus, Musæus, Homer, Archimedes, Dædalus, Thales, Plato, Lycurgus, Solon, Pythagoras, &c., had themselves initiated in these mysteries, which differed little in their liturgy, and not at all in their moral tendency, from the Dionysia.

Bacchus was surnamed Dionysus, derived from Διος (the genitive of Ζευς, Jupiter) and from Nysa, a town in which he is supposed to have been brought up. Several writers of antiquity have maintained that this god, undoubtedly the Theban one, was the same as Osiris, whilst Ceres, in whose honour the Eleusinian feasts were celebrated at Eleusis, was no other that the Egyptian Isis. However this may be (and mythology is often here at variance), it appears certain that the custom of the Dionysiac festivals, of Bacchanalia, was introduced from Egypt into Greece by a certain Melampus, the son of Amiathon. [1] He, according to Herodotus, introduced the worship of Bacchus and of the phallus into Greece.

The Athenians celebrated the festivals of Bacchus with the greatest splendour; and the Romans very soon introduced the Bacchanalia into the whole of Italy. Originally no men were admitted, and consequently the scandal was not very great; but afterwards, when men were introduced, these festivals degenerated into such atrocious orgies that the Senate thought it right to interfere. In the year of Rome 568 a decree was issued for the suppression of these scandals throughout Italy. [2]

The places where the Dionysia were by preference held were isolated spots; not only because the effrontery of the Bacchantes found encouragement in solitude, but also because they were more adapted to the echoing of the voice. "Evohe, evohe!" shouted Jupiter when encouraging his, son Bacchus to overcome the obstacles which the jealous Juno threw in his way, "Evohe, evohe!" repeated the eager actors in the scene. Hence the word Bacchanal is used to designate a great uproar or loud clamour.

The priestesses of Bacchus were fourteen in number; they were called Gerarai, from Gerasko (to grew old), because they were chosen when advanced in years. They had fourteen altars, and presided at the offering of fourteen sacrifices; they were the real Bacchantes, but subsequently the name was extended to all the females that took part in these outrageous scenes. Some authors have maintained that the Bacchantes were virgins, and continued to be so, defending themselves against all attacks amidst the most extravagant sensualities and Bacchantic libations.

The statue of the god was generally painted over with cinnibar, besides which it was clad in the skin of a stag, a panther, a leopard, or some other animal. The hierophant, or priest, upon whom devolved the duty of revealing sacred things, represented the Demiurgus, the Creator. The

---

[1] Herodotus II., § 49.

[2] Herodotus, ubi supra. Diodorus Siculus. Athenæus. Memoires do l'Academie des Inscriptions.

torch-bearers went by the name of Lampadophores; their chief personified the sun; the acolyte symbolised the moon, and the sacred herald Mercury. [1]

Processions, in which vessels filled with wine and covered with vine-branches were carried about, constituted the principal ceremonies. Then came the canephores, young women carrying baskets of flowers and fruit and after them the Lampadophores. These were followed by flute and cymbal players; after whom a multitude of men and women dressed up as satyrs, pans, fauns, sileni, nymphs, and bacchantes; crowned with violets and ivy-leaves, with dishevelled hair, flushed with the fumes of wine, their garments arranged with immodest art, so as to disclose to the eye what the eye should not have seen, they marched onward, singing the phallica, obscene songs in honour of Bacchus.

In the rear of this motley crowd came the Phallophores and Hyphalli, the former exhibiting shamelessly to the spectators images of the lingam, which by means of straps, were tied to the hip, and the latter carrying the same objects, but of more gigantic dimensions, at the end of a long pole. The whole procession was closed by the fourteen priestesses, whom the archon, or high priest, had entrusted with the preparatory arrangements.

In Egypt, the ceremony was very much the same, except that the Egyptians had invented, instead of a phallus, figures about two feet high, which they set in motion by a spring. These figures, of which the virile attribute was almost as large as the rest of the body, were moved up and clown with a string by the women, who carried them through the towns and villages. When the crowd had reached its destination, which was either the middle of a lonely forest or the enclosure of a deep valley surrounded by rocks, these debauched fanatics drew the image of Bacchus from a box which the Latins called the arca ineffabilis. It was then placed on a Hermes, and a swine was offered to the god as a holocaust, after which the wine and the fruit were liberally distributed among the crowd. In a very short time the plentiful libations, the continuous clamour, the immoderate hilarity, and the mingling of the sexes, produced a general excitement, and drove the priests of the infamous divinity to the highest pitch of frenzy. Every one behaved in the presence of all as if he were isolated from the whole world, and several hundreds of spectators witnessed the most disgraceful scenes

---

[1] EUSEBIUS, Catena Patrum, lib. III.

of debauchery. The naked women ran about exciting and inviting the men by obscene words and gestures, and the latter never thought of what had become in that crowd of their wives, their sisters, or their daughters. They little heeded the shame, which was reciprocal. In a word, there was no kind of licentiousness which was not improved upon on this occasion.

At last the night that had spread its veil over this scene of abomination fled before the car of Phœbus and the god was restored to the arca ineffabilis. The men staggering, filled with wine, and enervated by their lusts, returned to their deserted homes, where they were gradually joined by their wives and children, dishonoured and defiled.

The government of a civilized nation could not tolerate all this scandal. We have already seen that the Bacchanalia were prohibited by the Roman Senate.

The bas-relief which has furnished the subject of the above explanation is a good representation of a Dionysiac or Bacchanal. In the centre is the old Silenus, crowned with ivy, carrying a cup in one hand, and in the other a crown, the emblem of his Victory over the drinkers. He staggers. and would certainly fall to the ground but for two young fauns who support him. A Lampadophor and a Canephor are behind him. To his left may be perceived, in order of succession, a Bacchante, a female cymbal-player, a young boy carrying some of the instruments of initiation, an immodest phallophore fixing his strap, a female Satyr placing the pedum and the syrinx at the feet of Bacchus-Hermes, who may be recognised by his horns and by the stag's skin which envelopes his chest. In the corner appears the god Cupid, who seems to have come to take part in the festival. To the left of Silenus is a small altar, and on it a pine-apple, and a lighted torch has been prepared for the Sacrifice. A Bacchante, lying on a bear-skin, reclines voluptuously in an attitude which leaves but little doubt as to the cause of her exhaustion. In the background appears a Satyr, who, attracted by the noise, leaves his dwelling in order to share in the orgie. Finally, at the extremity of the bas-relief, a woman in the disguise of a Satyr places herself on the attribute of a Priapus-Hermes. The scene takes place in a forest, where may be seen several oaks and a palm-tree.

SACRIFICE TO PRIAPUS

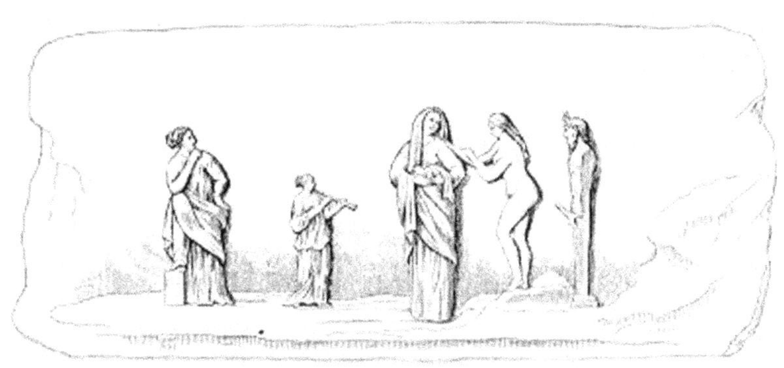

Plate VIII.

IN this bas-relief is represented one of the most disgraceful ceremonies of Paganism. Several women are conducting a young girl, whom we may suppose to be newly married, to a Statue of Priapus, and the unfortunate creature is already on the point of making to the marble figure the painful sacrifice of her virginity. She alone, of all the troop, is entirely naked; she bends her head with a confused and sad air, and leans on the shoulder of an aged woman, possibly her mother. Not far off a little girl plays on the double flute to stifle the cries of pain extorted from the victim; farther off an old woman, resting on one knee, looks upon the scene, and appears to grow impatient at the hesitation manifested by the young wife.

We have spoken in our introduction of these abominable sacrifices prevalent in ancient times. We do not consider them less revolting than those which stained with blood the dark thickets in which the Druids celebrated their mysteries. The latter coldly slaughtered men whom society had already doomed to death, extracting absurd presages from the groaning of their entrails and the palpitations of their tortured limbs. The former caused the purest blood of innocent virgins to flow on an obscene marble; without pity for the cries and torments of the youthful victims, they pitilessly destroyed that magic talisman which makes the married pair who have mingled together their first sentiments of desire, of shame, and of pleasure, so dear to each other.

It may nevertheless be presumed that this impure rite did not long subsist; but we may reasonably suppose that the priests of the false divinities then turned the public credulity to their own advantage, and themselves supplied the place of insensible idols.

In the temple of Isis at Pompeii, on an altar upon which the statue of the goddess was placed, may be seen a hollow pedestal, into which access was had by a concealed staircase, which terminated in the interior dwelling of the priests. It was by this passage that the impostor passed who was entrusted with the task of making the statues speak . . . . . . ab uno disce omnes. [1]

---

[1] The bas-relief here spoken of is in terra-cotta. It belongs to the cabinet of M. de S. C., who has been obliging enough to communicate it to us. The subject which it represents is repeated in one of the pieces belonging to the collection of the secret cabinet of the Royal Museum of Naples; but the limits within which we have been obliged to confine this work not having allowed us to give both, we have chosen this one as the more complete and ingenious of the two.

THE PHALLUSES IN STONE

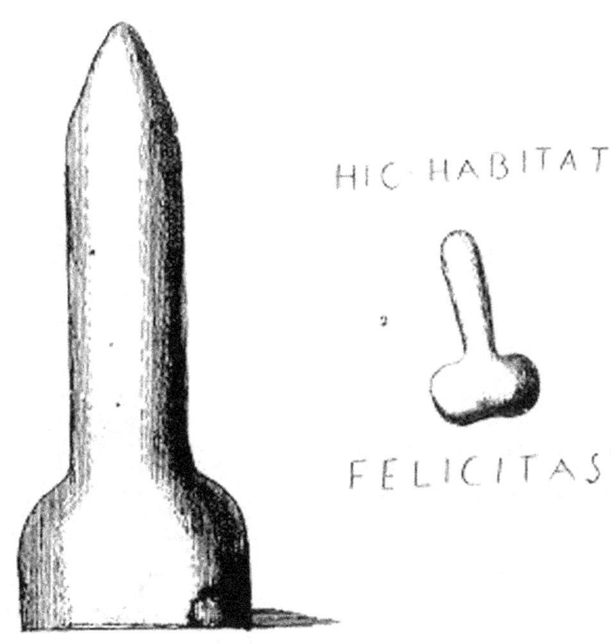

Plate IX.

IN certain towns, the corners of streets and the railings of public fountains may still be seen embellished with posts the form of which scarcely differs, except in the base, from the one here given. The habit of seeing them every day is alone the cause of their not being remarked; however, in those newly constructed, especially in the fine parts of Paris, a form has been adopted at once simpler and less indecorous.

Priapus was the protector of gardens; it was he who kept off the thieves from them. Devout persons thought it sufficient for that purpose to place his statue and attributes on the limits of their property; but a certain area of land could not have been protected equally on all sides by it small number of these statues, and the multiplication of them would have rendered the precaution too costly; their place was supplied by coarse images of the nature of that which is represented here.

As we have already said, the attributes of the garden god were accounted sure preservatives against the influence of evil-disposed persons, of magicians, and sorcerers; and this belief is still prevalent in the East, in Italy, and in Spain. It must not, then, be wondered at that at a period when this worship was freely admitted into the palaces of the great and rich, there should be found a humble artisan who had the notion of placing on his stall the protecting image of this singular god. Hic habitat felicitas, here happiness dwells; it is in the shelter of this revered image that we live exempt from trouble and care.

This stone was found at Pompeii, on the door of a baker's shop.

TWO LITTLE VOTIVE COLUMNS

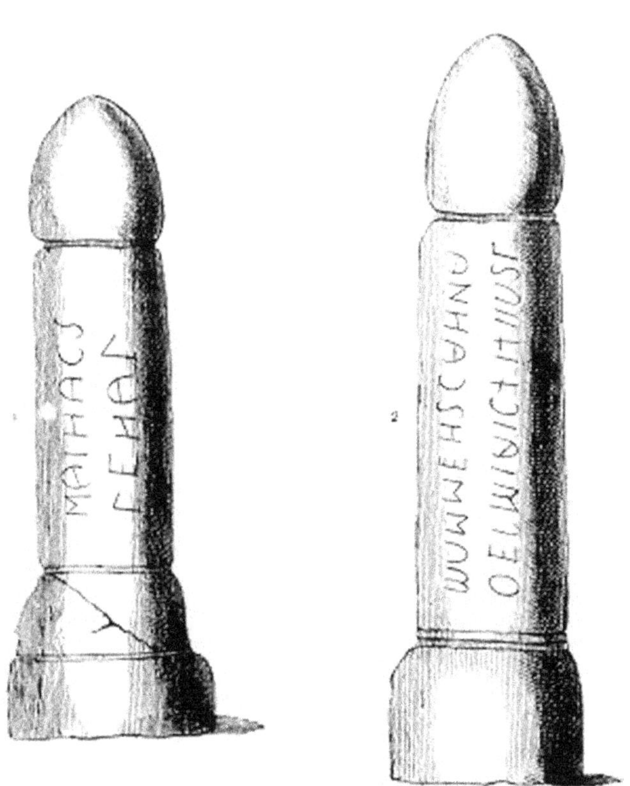

Plate X.

THESE votive columns, in the form of a phallus--strange monuments of a shameful worship--each bear an inscription in the Uscan language and character.

The Uscans were a people of Campania, between Capua and Naples they were so much given to sensual pleasures that their corruption became proverbial throughout Italy. This people instituted highly indecent games, and represented in Atella, one of their towns, certain plays, in which the recklessness of debauchery reached its culminating point; but the Romans, already very depraved themselves, gradually adopted these licentious performances, and called them from the name of the town, Atellania. The degradation of Uscan morals was not without its influence on the Greek language, which formed the basis of the vernacular of Campania: thus the Latins used Osce loqui to express both licentious language and obsolete phraseology. From the Latin Osoi, or Opsi, Obsci, is derived the word OBSCENE.

According to Silius Italicus, the country of the Uscans comprehended all the towns along the coast, between Terracina and Cumæ. The principal town was Capua, afterwards so famous for its pleasures, or rather debaucheries. This nation was destroyed, and the remnants of it became amalgamated with the neighbouring peoples; but for a long time the Uscan language was used in Rome for the obscene plays. All knowledge of this language has now entirely disappeared from the memory of man, and therefore the Uscan as well as the Etruscan inscriptions are for the most part indecipherable. Several antiquarians, among them the learned Montfaucon, have given their attention to the various transformations of the Greek characters from their Phœnician origin to their entire annihilation among the peoples of Italy. This, however, they could not do with the language. It would be in vain to find anything like pure characters in the Etruscan or Uscan inscriptions through the aid of Greek palæography, because the interpretation of the words would not the less, in most cases, be impossible.

Figure 1. represents merely two words; having regard to a certain resemblance of characters, we might perhaps there recognize the inscription To the Son of Maia. This is therefore most likely a votive monument to Mercury, but we do not desire to overrate the weight of this hypothesis. It appears, however, that the second word begins with ΓΕΗ, derived from γῆ, earth, root of generation; to engender, to produce, γείνομαι.

DRILLOPOTA

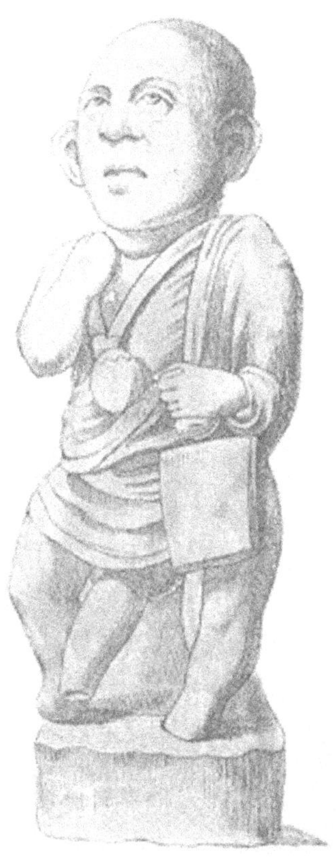

PLATE XI.

THIS grotesque little figure was found at Civita.[1] It represents one of those unfortunate beings whose only purpose in life seems to be as a kind of plaything to their fellow-creatures. What have they done to deserve the

---

[1] A town of Naples, near Cassano, in the northern part of Calabria.

worst share in the distribution of the common heritage, those sad abortions of a capricious mother? Unfathomable Providence! here too, undoubtedly, we should have cause to wonder at Thy will, if Thy motive were known; but it is not given to man to read Thy sacred pages; he knows that the truth exists, he feels it, but he knows it not.

As it was the custom only a short time ago in several courts of Europe, so in antiquity the wealthy had certain dwarfs in their service, whose business it was to amuse the company when dull. They had to dance on the table, and were shut up in gigantic pasties. They poured out wine for their masters, and followed them when they went out. They were called moriones, from μωρὸς, a fool, and morus, a word used by Plautus; or fatui, whence our word fatuous comes; and sometimes insani, nugatores, &c.

These buffoons were in the habit of shaving their heads to make themselves appear still more ridiculous. The present figure is entirely bald: near his left arm are the tavolæ pugillares, tablets which the children used at school. He wears round his neck the golden ball (bulla), which distinguished the sons of the nobles and senators. The origin of this distinction dates from Tarquin the Elder, who awarded this mark of honour to his son for having conquered his opponent in single combat. [1] The bulla could be opened at pleasure, and was used to keep talismans in.

The tunic of this singular personage is raised, and reveals a phallus of enormous proportions. This agrees with the assertion of Theophrastus, that the membrum of dwarfs was out of all proportion with their body; that is to say, that the former was just as large as the latter was diminutive. [2]

Καὶ Θεόφραστος ὡς νάννον αἰδοῖον ἔχοντα
μεγα, οἱ γὰρ νάννοι μέγα αἰδοῖον ἔχουσι· [3]

---

[1] Pliny, xxiii. 1.

[2] The drilled vessel behind this figure represents one of those drinking-cups called drillopota, of which we shall speak when explaining another plate.

[3] SUIDAS.--HESYCHIUS.

DRILLOPOTA

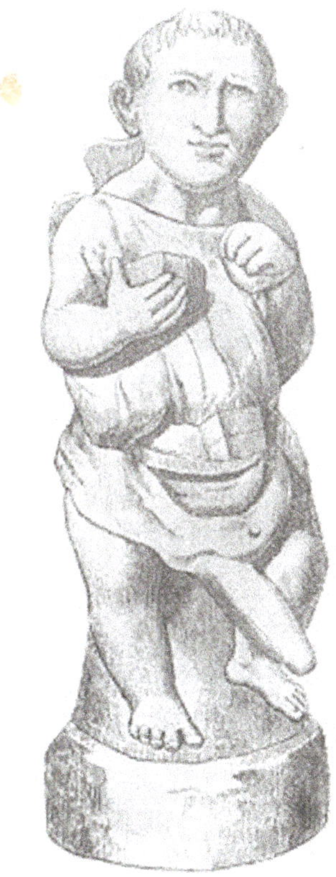

PLATE XII.

BEHIND this figure is seen a vessel, which represents one of those obscene vases called Drillopotæ, [1] out of which the ancients were wont to drink on certain occasions, undoubtedly in honour of Venus,

---

[1] From δρῖλος, the virile member, and ποτήρ, a drinking-cup.

or perhaps of Bacchus; for, assuredly it would be difficult to suppose anything like dignity or seriousness in such ceremonies. For a long time the corruption of the antique nations led them to feign a disgraceful attachment for the immodest ceremonies to which they were no longer able to yield a sincere worship.

This dwarf holds two objects in his hand which it would be difficult to qualify--two lumps of bread, perhaps. He carries in his belt a sort of casket, which may be the crepundia, a small box or purse for children to keep their toys in.

This Drillopota comes from Civita.

DRILLOPOTA

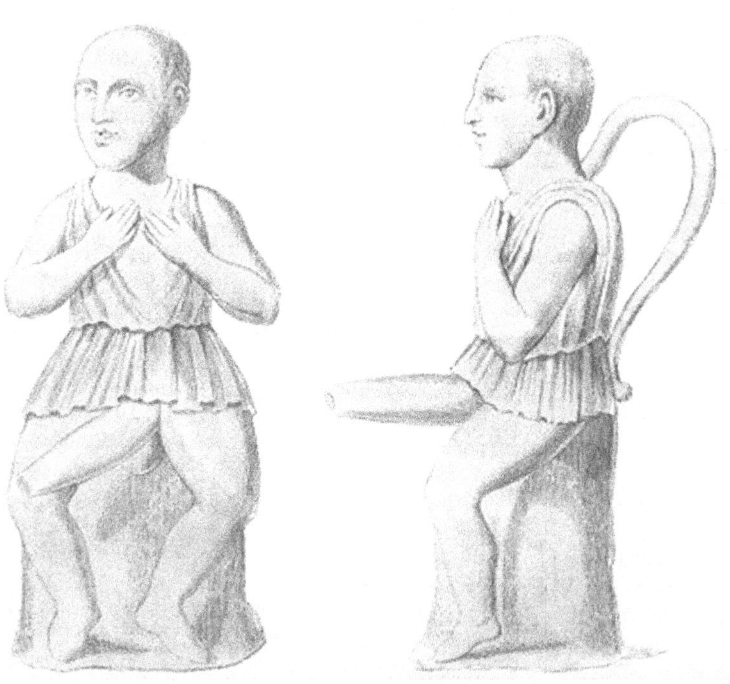

PLATE XIII.

LIKE the former, this is another specimen of the drillopotæ, representing a dwarf, a child's body with the head of an old man. Its figure is as much out of proportion as its attitude is obscene and yet its gestures seem too indicate modesty.

Sometimes the ancients made use of certain drillopotæ, made of glass these were called phallovitroboli, or phalloveretroboli, drinking-glasses in the form of phalluses. [1] Juvenal says: "He drinks from a Priapeian glass;" [2] and the commentator adds: "Glass phalluses called drillopotæ."

The present vase is seen full and side-face; it will be remarked that the upper part has no opening, whence it appears that the vessel was turned upside down and filled at the bottom; it is probable that they drank from he projecting part as from a spout. O tempora!!

Many other drillopotæ have been found at Civita, Herculaneum, and several parts of Magna Grecia; but as they are not in any way different from those we have described, we have deemed it useless to repeat a description of them.

---

[1] PLINY, xxxiii. 1.
[2] JUVENAL, Sat. ii. 95.

DANCER TO THE CROTALUM

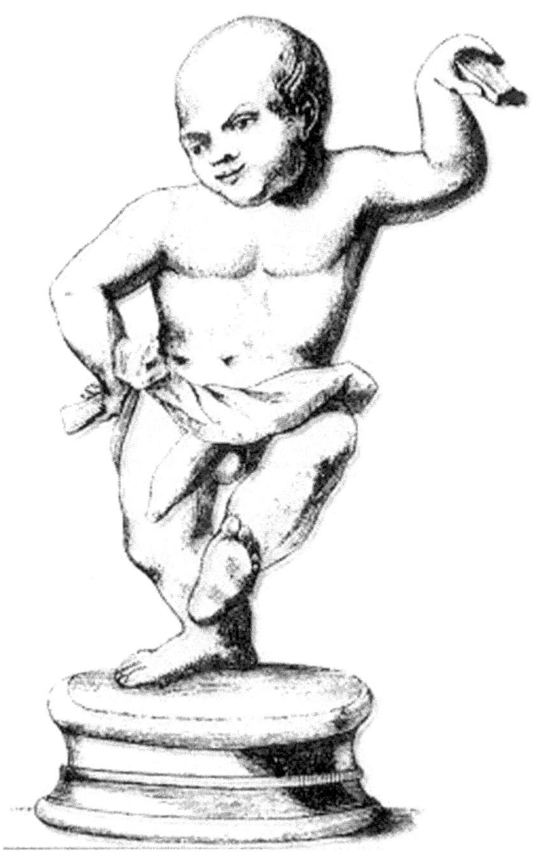

Plate XIV.

WE have spoken in the explanation of Plate XI. of the moriones, or fatui, of whom this dancer in bronze is one. He is entirely naked, the girdle round his loins being, altogether insufficient to conceal his enormous parts.

He is dancing to the sound of the crotalum. This was a kind of cymbal made of wood, of terra cotta, or of metal, which almost produced the sound of the Spanish castanets. It was consecrated to Priapus, and used in lascivious dances,

Copa syrisca caput graia redimita mitella
Crispum sub crotalo docta movere latus.

VIRGIL, Copa.

Cymbala cum crotalis prurientiaque arma Priapo
Ponit, et adducta tympana pulsa manu.

Priapeia, Ep. 26.

This little statue is by no means badly executed; the dancer's pose sufficiently shows how grotesque, ridiculous, and obscene such dances were. The statuary took his model from life; one of those wretches whose occupation was to divert their lords and masters. The more natural they were in their vulgarity, and the more vulgar in their naturalness, the more they were appreciated:--

Morio dictus erat, viginti millibus emi;
Redde mihi nummos, Gargiliane, sapit.

Martial Epig. viii. 13.

A PRIAPUS-HERMES

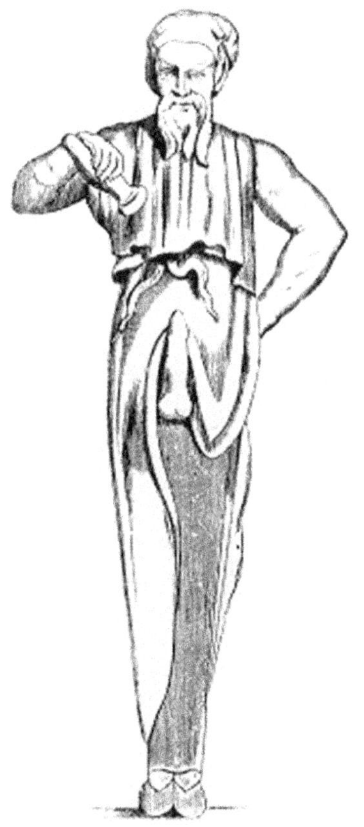

Plate XV.

NO doubt this bronze, which was found at Portici, must have belonged to a votive chapel. It represents an old man whose beard is carefully combed; his ears, of considerable dimensions, resemble those of a faun. He is clad in the dress called talare, tied round his loins. His legs seem set in a sheath, and his feet are shod; his tunic is turned up; his left hand rests on his hip, and with his right hand he pours the contents of a vase of essences on his phallus. This part of the statue is out of all proportion. The vase is supposed to contain one of those compounds to which was attributed the property of restoring to the athletes of Venus their pristine vigour.

The ancients delighted in mixing aphrodisiac beverages, or what were held as such, to which the Greeks gave the name of satyrion.

Theophrastus, Dioscorides, and Pliny [1] speak complacently of the essences and ointments which had the property of giving extraordinary Vigour to the male.

It appears, according to these authors, that the tubercles of the orchis hircina served as the basis of aphrodisiac preparations. The enchantresses of Thessaly dissolved fresh tubercles of this plant in goat's milk, and thus produced a beverage which they gave to worn-out old men to rekindle the flames of love in them. On the other hand, in order to produce a contrary effect and to extinguish immoderate fires, they made use of tubercles, which being upwards of a year old, were withered and dry. If we may credit the mythologists, it was by the aid of such an ingredient that Hercules, having received the hospitality of Thespius, showed his gratitude to him by ravishing the fifty daughters of his good host in a single night. Proculus, having taken a hundred young virgins prisoners, deflowered them all round in fifteen days. A King of India, named Androphilus, having sent to Antiochus a plant of the satyrion species, Theophrastus declares that the slave entrusted with this wonderful product boasted of having, by its means offered seventy sacrifices to Venus in succession. [2]

The Egyptians call a plant which they consider as aphrodisiac, chan-lendjâam-dgarbi. This is the maranta-galanga of Linnæus.

Only a few years ago there were still to be found in the pharmacopoeia electuaries and preparations supposed to possess the same property. In the first rank there figured a kind of lizard, a native of Africa, the scincus officinalis. Taken in the form of powder, it was considered as a powerful

---

[1] THEOPH. Op.; DISCOR. iii. 134; Pliny xxvi. 10.
[2] THEOPHR. Hist. ix. 19.

auxiliary in amorous combats. The merchant ships returning from Alexandria to Marseilles brought back bottles of them, in which these animals were packed together like anchovies.

Cantharides, truffles, aromatics, several species of mushrooms, and in particular one description, are looked upon as aphrodisiacs. Monsieur Descourtilz, in speaking of the last-named mushroom, in his "Picturesque Flora of the Antilles, says:--"Careful housewives give their lovers plenty of it to eat, as an erotic incentive." And further on he adds: "This species is looked upon as an aphrodisiac, and matrons do not fail to garnish with it the dishes of young adepts whom they destine to the first sacrifice to Venus and to revive the torpid spirit of old stagers who can do nothing but exhibit the same inefficiency over and over again. The pimento, nutmeg, clove, cinnamon, and ginger mixed with it, add to the aphrodisiac virtue of this extraordinary mushroom, and the whole would almost raise a dead man from his grave." [1]

Whatever may be the virtue of these preparations, we can only deplore the infatuation of those unhappy persons who venture to have recourse to them. The use of these factitious means, and the venereal excesses they

---

[1] A story is related, on this subject, of two young girls, fast linked in friendship who were married on the same day. In a moment of enthusiasm, they pledged themselves on oath to tell each other every morning the number of amorous tributes paid them by their husbands during the night. And so they did. On the morning after their nuptials, the newly-married women, who lived opposite each other, stood at their respective windows, and exchanged the signs they had agreed upon between them. With an air radiant with gladness, the first lifted both hands and showed ten fingers. The second, blushing and with a drooping head, showed only one "Poor child," exclaimed her neighbour to herself, p. 35 I pity you indeed to be so badly matched." The following day the same scene took place, at which the happier of our belles showed only nine fingers, whilst the other still showed only one. On the third day the first showed eight, on the fourth seven, on the fifth six, and on the sixth five, and so on, descending in proportion every day, whilst her neighbour still continued to show only one finger. These manœuvres lasted as long as the happier one had something to show and to boast of, but she shortly after discontinued, and showed her friend only her clenched hands, a sign of anger as well as impotency, The other, however, now raised her head proudly, for she was at least able to show that her daily allowance was still being supplied her with the most scrupulous exactitude.

cause, cannot but lead in a very short time from satiety to despair, and from despair to death.

Temperance and sobriety can alone defer the term when our amorous combats must cease.

NOTE.--There exists in the same museum another statuette similar in everything but the base to that we have just described.

VOTIVE FIGURE

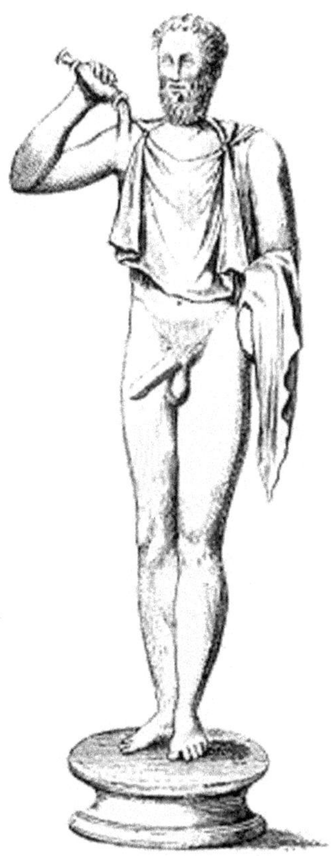

Plate XVI.

AN old man, whose left hand is enveloped in the chlamys, after the manner of athletes, pours on his phallus the liquor contained in a vase of elegant form.

Here, as perhaps in the preceding plate, the allegorical meaning constitutes one of the most important degrees of initiation into the mysteries of Isis and Osiris, of Bacchus or of the Sun. Ablution was a symbol dear to the ancients; it indicated at one and the same time the union of water and fire, at the period when baths are necessary to temper the ardour of the latter. Thence, as we have already said, is derived the origin of the fires of the festival of St John, and of the sprinklings of cold water still in use at that period of the year in some parts of France.

In the application, the positive meaning is, we think, the representation of a custom very common among the Romans. [1] The vase which the old man holds in his right hand is supposed to contain an aphrodisiac essence: and indeed it may be remarked that figures of this kind all represent old men, the young not needing to have recourse to these irritant preparations in order to prepare themselves for the act of coition.

To the details we have given on this subject in the preceding article, we may add the following:

Antony, having become desperately enamoured of Cleopatra, fell for some time into a strange dilemma. The excesses in which he had at first indulged in the arms of his royal mistress had weakened him to such a degree as to disable him for a long time from satisfying her ever-impetuous and ever-increasing desires. And assuredly Cleopatra was, both by temperament and habit, the least likely woman in the World to content herself with a meagre ration. History has preserved the remembrance of the truly prodigious prowess of this celebrated woman: "In one night, having assumed a veil, she lay with a hundred and six men in a public brothel."

Antony, on hearing of the numerous infidelities of his mistress, became greatly enraged, and even threatened to destroy her if she did not alter her behaviour. Cleopatra, terrified, resigned herself to abstinence, but at the expense of her health. She fell so dangerously ill that Antony, in despair, thought it his duty to apply forthwith to Quintus Soranus, a learned doctor and grave philosopher. He laid before him, with great frankness, the causes of the malady which was ravaging the beautiful Cleopatra, importunately entreating him to point out both the means of tempering the ardour which internally devoured the passionate Queen, and those of reviving in himself desire and vigour. Quintus Soranus justified the confidence reposed in him

---

[1] See the explanation of Plate XV.

by the Consul, and wrote him a letter on the subject, which Latin antiquity has preserved for us, and which contains the following passages:--

"Touched with your troubles, as a devoted friend should be, I have long sought by what means I could alleviate, or even entirely destroy, the anxiety you have confessed to me. I have consulted several books, and interrogated the secrets of nature, both in the class of animals, in that of stones, of trees, and of herbs; and although I found many remedies to cool the ardours of lust, I did not, however, discover the means of extinguishing the fire of libertinism, until at last, in following out my researches to the temple of Venus in the island of Scio, I found there a book which contained the veritable recipe, and the virtue of this ointment I now send you, as also some other preparations preserved for the use of women; you will be able to judge of its efficacy both by what I tell you and by your own experience. The virtue of this ointment is such that any woman feels herself so absorbed in the love of the man who makes use of it, in holding intercourse with her, that the memory of every other passion immediately vanishes. This is the way in which you must at first proceed: Abstain during nine days from all venereal labour, so as to lose none of your strength. Make use of warm aliments, as also of cheese, eggs, strong wine, and spices. If you were old, or your temperament naturally cold, I might point out to you the stimulants used in medicine; but as you have no need of them, you can make use of ordinary meat. What you must especially attend to, in the next place, is that, after the ninth day, when you prepare yourself for the amorous combat, your instrument shall not be less than ten inches long. If you cannot obtain this naturally, you must do it by means of art."

THE HERMES IN BRONZE

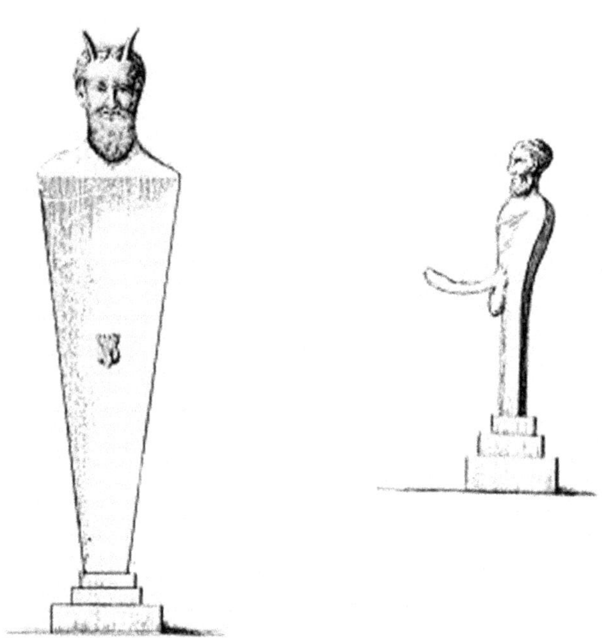

Plate XVII.

AN old man, whose left hand is enveloped in the chlamys, after the manner of athletes, pours on his phallus the liquor contained in a vase of elegant form.

No. 2 is a grotesque figure, representing the same god.

It cannot be doubted that these little bronze figures were the household gods of some Roman family. A great many of them have been found, but as they differ but little from each other, it is useless to describe them all.

It may be remarked that the custom of worshipping unworthy divinities was not merely confined to the ancient world. Thus, for instance (if we may believe Garcilasso de la Vega), in Mexico there were temples consecrated to the gods of drunkenness, lechery, theft, &c. In fact, the Mexicans had their Bacchus, their Priapus, and their Mercury. This may serve as a confirmation of what we maintained in the Introduction to this book, that, as soon as man emerged from the savage state, his first religious promptings were directed towards the adoration of the mysterious powers which tend to the propagation of the human species. The Mexicans also worshipped the the sun, and with all the nations of antiquity the sun was the principle of fire. Fire was looked upon as the principle of generation-the reproductive power, and the genitals as the attributes of the fertilising divinity of nature. All these, ideas were mixed together in one common belief, and gave rise to the same identical forms of worship.

THE TRIPOD

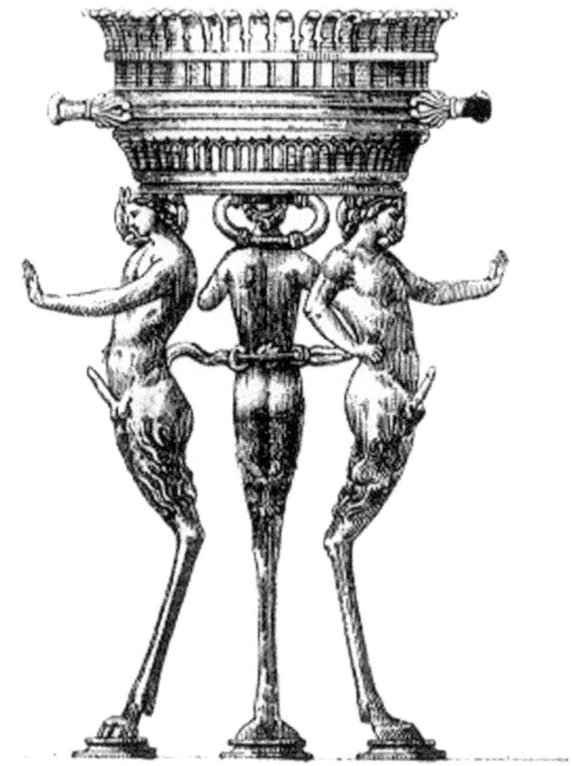

Plate XVIII.

HIS wonderful tripod was found in a votive chapel at Herculaneum. The gracefully-formed corbel is supported by three exquisitely-finished figures: satyrs with their members erect. They are resting their right hands on their hips, and closing their middle fingers in token of silence. They stretch forward their left hands, as if to keep off the profane, who must not take part in the sacrifice. Their tails are gracefully entwined round the central ring.

The elegance and perfection of this bronze place it among the most precious treasures of this mine of antiquities. It would be difficult to say to which divinity it is consecrated; for the phalluses, the object of which was to drive away earthly impurities, and to keep off evil spirits in the solemn performance of a sacrifice, occur indiscriminately in the temples of Jupiter, Apollo, Mercury, Bacchus, Priapus, Venus, &c.

Tripods, the origin of which is lost in the remotest ages, were consecrated in most of the ancient forms of worship. As a rule, those initiated in the mysteries of Delphi, Isis, and Eleusis offered a tripod in token of their devotion.

The ternary number, which recurs everywhere throughout Nature, physically and morally, played a prominent part in the pagan rites.[1] It embraced the divinities of air, earth, and water, of which Jupiter, Neptune, and Pluto were the lords, and which were indiscriminately called Zeus, the Supreme Divinity. The Muses numbered three times three: there were three Graces, three Furies, three Fates, three Hecates, a Cerberus with three heads, &c.

---

[1] As also in Judaism, Buddhism, Brahminism, and Christianity.

TWO MIMIC BUFFOONS

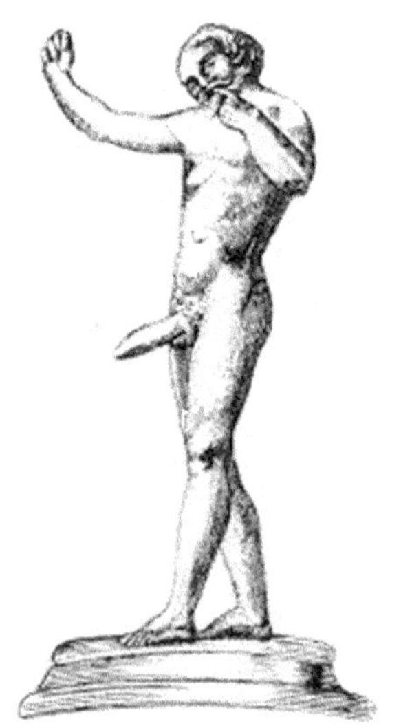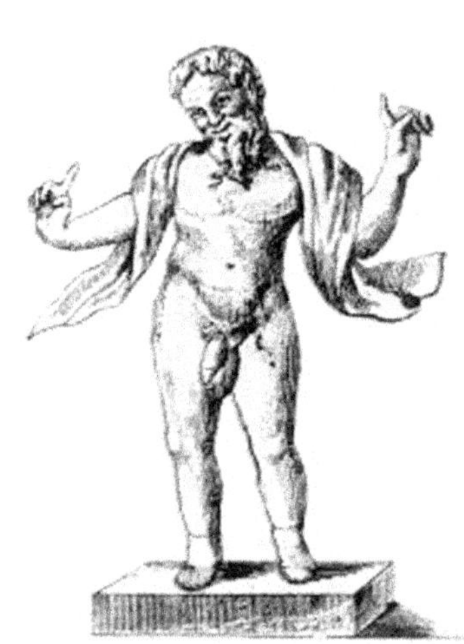

Plate XIX.

GOOD in execution, this little bronze represents one of those buffoons whom the Latins called sanniones. Their occupation was to create laughter with the aid of pantomime. The present one is entirely nude, and displays a phallus of gigantic proportions. His bald and bearded head inclines above his right shoulder. He is making an expressive grimace, and carrying the fore finger of his left hand to his mouth. His other hand is closed, with the exception of the thumb, which is passed between the fore and middle finger. This indecent gesture is still in our own day called "making the fig." The expression is common in early every country of Europe. In England the phrase "don't care a fig" is well known, and Shakespeare speaks of the "Italian Ficco" more than once. Nurses now-a-days may often be seen threatening children with the sign, little thinking of the origin and true meaning of the symbol.

To Mercury was consecrated the first fig--and to Priapus the virginity of a young girl. Is this analogy the origin of the denomination given to this immodest gesture?

The ancient Southern peoples, and especially the Greeks, held pantomime in high esteem. The art was transmitted to the Romans, and perpetuated through all the south of Europe; it is especially carried to a great point of perfection in Sicily and Naples. At Naples, the stage understands how to turn to profit the theory of the art of pantomime. The Neapolitan punchinello is entrusted with the principal part. This character, of which the type is the "laughing, censorship of manners," is of the greatest antiquity, and the little figure we are explaining may be considered as a veritable punchinello; for irk all times, and among all nations, persons have been found who, under the mask of buffoonery, have arrogated to themselves the right of saying anything and everything.

As for the particular and local character of the Neapolitan punchinello, his origin may be said to date from the middle ages. At the time when the House of Anjou occupied the throne, there was a French governor at Naples, of sombre and atrabilious mood. He had in his service a domestic born at Acerra, a little town situated on the western side of Mount Vesuvius, whose inhabitants still dress like the punchinello, that is to say, wearing a Calabrian hat of the shape of a sugar-loaf and without any brim, their only clothing being drawers of commodious width and a shirt above, bound round the loins in the form of a blouse.

This servant was called Paolo Ciniello. He was a buffoon, witty, gluttonous, and cowardly. His master was very fond of his repartees, which were full of naïveté, wit, and good sense. In moments of ill-humour he was in the habit of calling for him, and not being able to repeat his name except with great difficulty, he called him Poulchinelle, of which the Italians made Pulcinella.

No. 2, a little figure in bronze, found at Pompeii, is another mimic-buffoon who is balancing his head and arms with great nonchalance, after this manner of the Chinese pagods. His two forefingers are stretched out, and seem to form a pair of horns.

TWO IDOLS

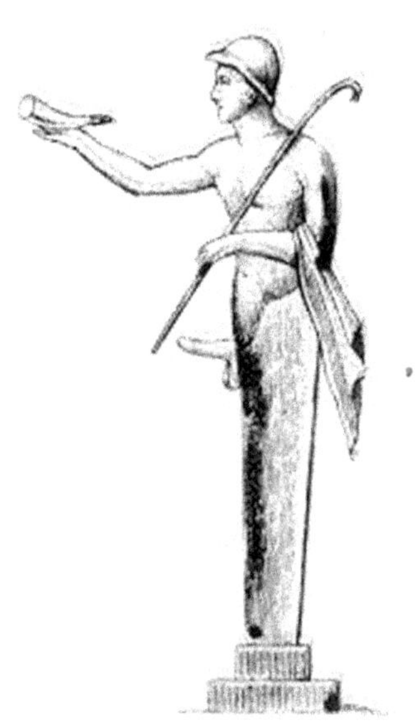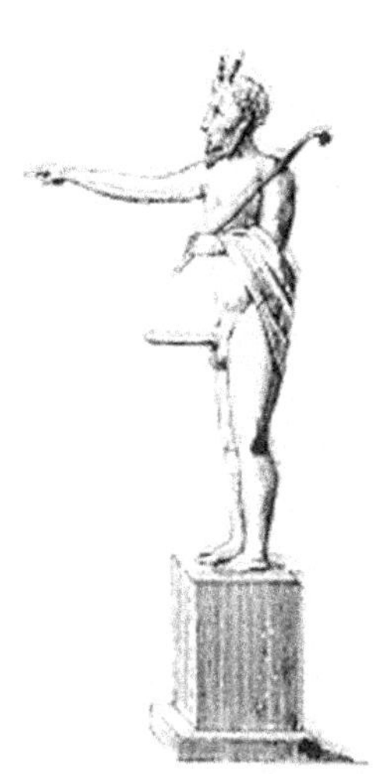

Plate XX.

NO. 1 is a little Hermes bearing the chlamys, the pedum, or pastoral hook the pedum, and the rhyton, the horn of an animal, which the ancients used to drink out of.

Athenæus [1] speaks of these horns, and also adds that wooden ones were made.

---

[1] ATHENÆUS, xi. 7.

No. 2 is a bearded and homed Faun also bearing the chlamys and the pedum. His right arm is raised horizontally, and his forefinger is stretched out in sign of command.

Of this sort of little idols there have been found, in the excavations of Pompeii and Herculaneum, a number almost equal to that of the little figures that come to us from Egypt. Their repetition would be tedious and unnecessary.

THREE BRONZE FIGURES

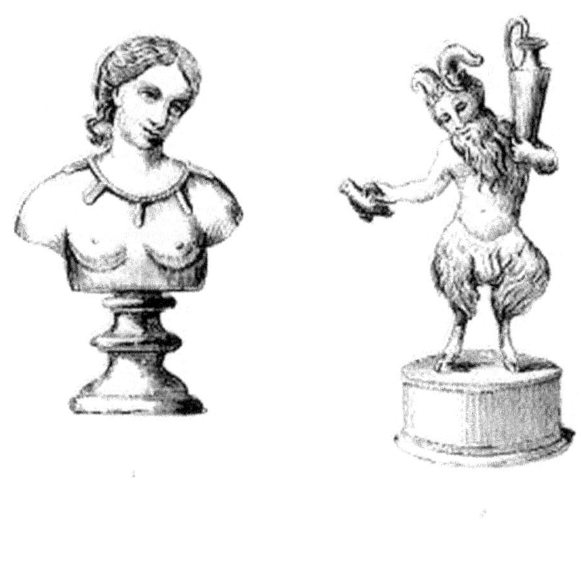

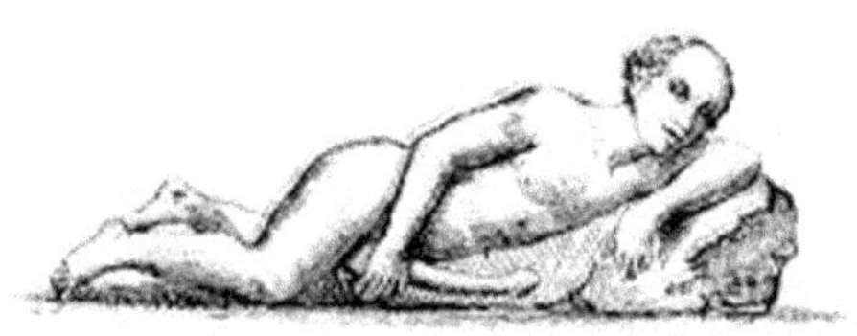

Plate XXI.

SEVERAL phalluses are suspended to a necklace round the neck of the first figure--a charming little bust of a woman. We have already said that among the Egyptians, and in Greece and Italy, the gravest matrons did not blush to wear these amulets in public. It was especially for barren women, and for those who generally brought forth children with difficulty and miscarriage, that these charms were reserved; but some only saw in these trinkets a kind of votive offering displaying the image of Priapus as many times as the god had satisfied their desires. "The unwearied Messalina lay with many men in one night. From none did she require any reward that he did not bring of his own free will. When day returned, the conqueress dedicated four-and-twenty wreaths of rose and myrtle to Priapus, Marsyas, and other mirthful deities: each being a thank-offering for a victory." [1]

Were it not for the undeniable monuments that antiquity has bequeathed to us, we should be led to believe that civilized nations have at all times had the same ideas as ourselves about decency, so natural does it appear not to separate mystery from the pleasures of the senses--unless we would become like the beasts! It was not so, however; and the countries that gave birth to Socrates, Plato, Lycurgus, Cicero, and Antoninus were sullied by the most dissolute manners and the most disgusting orgies. Some centuries have elapsed since a religion of purity and chastity struck its powerful roots into the soil of old Europe, and yet some traces are still to be found there of the infamous worship of the god Phallus. Even in France, a country which for a long time past has marched in the van of civilization, later centuries have witnessed public processions in which, out of devotion, men who called themselves flagellants appeared entirely naked!

No. 2 represents a satyr, perhaps the god Pan, whose head is surmounted by an enormous pair of horns. A long beard flows over his chest. In one hand he holds an amphora, full, doubtless, of wine:

"For Venus would freeze if unaided by Bacchus and Ceres."

With the other he holds by its wings a bird, which Sylvain Maréchal, and the academicians of Naples before him, have declared to be a cock, but which nowise resembles that animal. Its size would lead us to take it for a pigeon or a turtle, and its shape for a sparrow. All these birds, whose loves are renewed several times in the year, are very lascivious: they were therefore consecrated to Venus.

It is to be presumed that this little figure was one of the household gods of a Roman dwelling: his large horns and immoderate phallus served to keep off sorceries. Let us remark in passing that, whatever may have been said

---

[1] Joannes Meursius.

on the subject, the custom of insulting husbands deceived by their wives by imagining them to have horns is merely derived from that very ancient, but yet very false opinion, that of the two men he is the happier whose wife is unfaithful; for the need she experiences, at every moment of the day, to lull to sleep the suspicions of him whom she is outraging, induces her incessantly to feign sweetness, resignation-all the virtues, in short, which she no longer possesses; besides that, her libertinism is sometimes only the result of ambition, and thus procures in the family an case and affluence which, without her, it would never know. Whilst the husband whose wife is virtuous must, they say, pay with usury for the sacrifices his companion imposes on herself through love of honesty. He is indeed to be pitied, whilst the former is as happy as if he wore horns; for horns, like phalluses, have the property of keeping off witchcraft and incantations, and incessantly bringing down joy, riches, and tranquillity. We have said, in the introduction to this work, that the superstition relative to horns still exists in all its vigour in the south of Italy, in Spain, and in the Levant.

It forms no part of our plan to demonstrate how absurd and immoral is the opinion which makes a deceived husband a happy man, and a respected husband an unfortunate being. Greatly to be pitied are those whose own hearts will not suggest to them all that we omit here! Truly those are to be pitied who cannot appreciate all the respect and consolation that there is in the pride of a woman who has nothing to reproach herself with, who can carry her head high everywhere; who, in fine, is not afraid, when necessary, to interpose between a guilty son and an angry husband, because she knows that son is no stranger in the family, and that he has a right to the paternal condescension!

The third figure is that of a bald old man lying on the ground. He is entirely naked, his right hand rests on a large erect phallus, and his left arm is passed under his head. As there existed in Kircher's museum a statue of the Indian Buddha, very nearly similar to this figure, with the Latin inscription, "DIVO MERCURIO" (to the god Mercury), certain Neapolitan antiquaries have believed that this also was the Indian Buddha, the ninth incarnation of Vishnu, the Greek Mercury, the Thoth of the Egyptians, &c., and what gives some weight to this opinion is that this piece comes from Egypt.

A VOTIVE PHALLUS

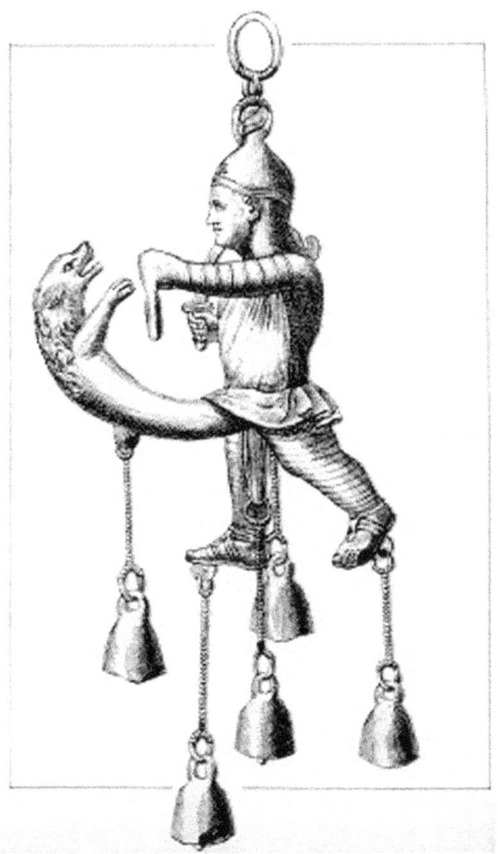

Plate XXII.

ONE of these symbolical figures to which the ancients ascribed the property of keeping off evil is shown here. They suspended them at the, entrance of shops, under the peristyles of houses, in bedrooms, or in the venereum. Sometimes these bronzes were used as lamps.

A gladiator covered with complete armour, his right hand grasping curved sword, appears to be endeavouring to entrap his enemy in a net which envelops his left hand; this was the manner of fighting with he gladiators called retiarii. His adversary is a furious animal, resembling a dog or a hyena, whose head serves as a crown to the enormous phallus of our gladiator. It is evidently an image of the combat which the strong and wise man wages with his warring senses.

To this figure are suspended five little bells. We have said in out Introduction that these instruments were considered as talismans against evil. But here they can only serve as a symbol of the triumph which the gladiator is about to obtain. We know indeed that the ancients, and especially the Romans, compelled the conquered and the slaves who followed the car of the conqueror to carry little bells, which the Latins called tintinnabula.

PHALLUS-HERMES

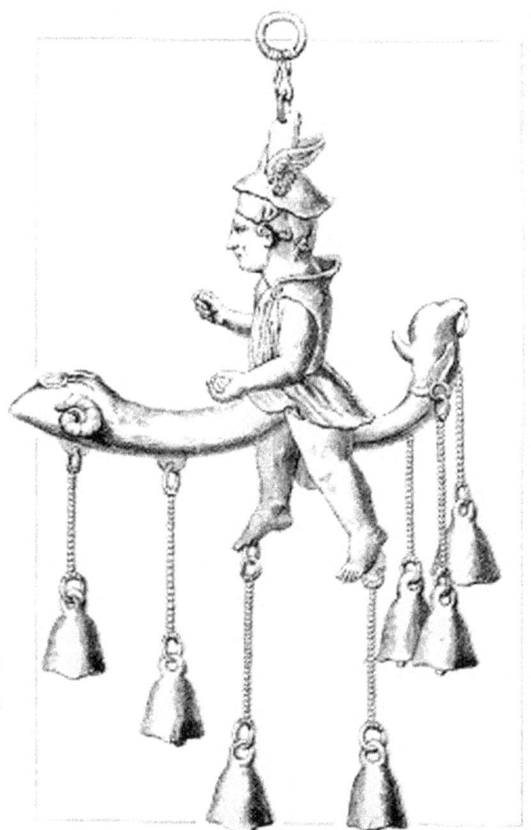

Plate XXIII.

THIS bronze seems to have been used as a lamp. A Hermes, with the petasus on his head, in a threatening attitude and with clenched fists, seems animated by a violent passion of anger or concupiscence. His tunic is raised by a phallus of gigantic proportions, terminating in the head of a he-goat.

The he-goat, of which the ancients had remarked the lasciviousness, was consecrated to Priapus.

This lamp is especially remarkable for a triple phallus attached to the posterior part of our Hermes.

Mercury (or Hermes) was one of the most immodest of the pagan gods. It was to him that Jupiter entrusted his amorous messages. He was in general the procurer of the gallant inhabitants of Olympus.

He had many temples, and his statue was rarely clad with any more decency than that of Priapus himself.

VOTIVE PHALLUS

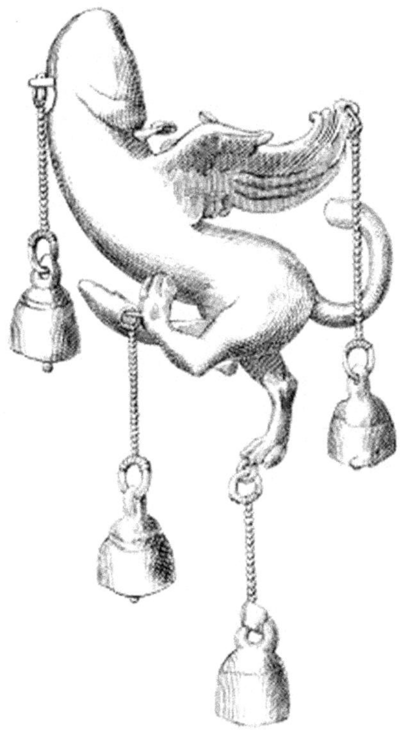

Plate XXIV.

THIS curious bronze, from the Borgia museum, represents a votive phallus under the form of a winged lion, bearing two other phalluses, of which one, serves as a tail. The hind part is terminated by two feet, one of which is lifted to the belly. On the back of the bronze we remark a ring, which was used to suspend it. We have also on this phallus four little bells attached to the same number of small chains.

We have here the symbols of force, rapidity, and triumph, which were characteristic among the ancients of the worship of the phallus. The same attributes belonged to certain other divinities, whose worship consisted chiefly in mysterious and symbolical practices: such were Bacchus, the Sun, Apollo, Osiris, so often and perhaps so justly confounded, Eros, Vesta, the Eleusinian Ceres, &c.! Such was also the god Mythra, for this divinity was no other than that of Eleusis. [1]

We are indebted for some curious notions concerning the worship of Mythra to the important researches of M. Felix Lajard and of M. von Hammer. We will take this opportunity to give a few details respecting the god Mythra, for the origin of his worship, and of those we have mentioned above--however different they may appear--unite in the one principle of generation.

According to Herodotus, Mythra is no other than the celestial Venus, or Love, the principle of generation and fecundity. In several eastern dialects Mythra signifies both light and love. The Persians received this worship from the Indians, and transmitted it to the people of Cilicia. Plutarch informs us that some pirates from that coast introduced it into Rome sixty-eight years before Christ.

According to Von Hammer, Mythra was not the Sun itself, but he was the genius of it, the ized. The name of this genius, which the Greeks wrote Mythras, is Mihr, and this word, adds the learned Orientalist, still signifies in modern Persian the ized, the sun, and love.

The worship of Mythra was free from the orgies which sullied at Rome even that of Isis and Eleusis.

"The mysteries of Mythra," says Von Hammer, "like the mysteries of Eleusis and others, afforded paganism a last retreat, in which it took shelter to defend itself against the ever-growing power of the Christian religion. The most enlightened and skilful defenders of paganism opposed to the Christian doctrine the mysteries of Isis and Eleusis, and especially those of Mythra, as a religious system superior to Christianity, of which the latter

---

[1] See Les Mythriaques, a treatise by M. von Hammer, with notes by Mr. Spencer Smith. See also an excellent dissertation by M. Denne-Baron, printed in La France Litteraire, vol. 9, p. 5.

contained in their opinion only false or partial revelations; the mysteries of Mythra were, in this respect, infinitely superior weapons to those of the other mysteries, since they were connected immediately with the religion of Zoroaster, which in so many points presents the nearest approach to the dogmas and rites of Christianity."

"The resemblance between the practices and ceremonies of the mysteries of Mythra and those of the Christian religion is admitted by the fathers of the Church, such as Justin and Tertullian; and the manner in which others, such as Gregory of Nazianzen and Jerome, expressed themselves concerning the mysteries of Mythra, sufficiently shows the importance they attached to this rivalry of practices and ceremonies. The establishment of Christianity was therefore doubtless one of the principal causes of the success and development of the worship of Mythra in the Roman empire, until it succumbed before the triumph of the Christian religion."

We see, then, from the above remarks, that the religion of Zoroaster, of which the Zendavesta, the living fire, is the Bible, gave birth to the mysteries of Mythra and to the ceremonies of Christianity; but in the latter case the rites have been sanctified, and, after the example of Tertullian and Saint Augustine, the admission may fearlessly be made.

Returning now to the plate which forms the subject of this explanation, we would remark that this figure has a direct relation with Mythra, the emblem and the genius of the Sun. An eagle and a lion, the Sun darts forth from the East, bears down all obstacles, hovers under the vault of the heavens, and descends to the horizon again, after receiving the homage of men. With the Egyptians the griffin was the emblem of the Sun and of Osiris.

Thus the fecundating principle is the divinity that presides over all the forms of worship in antiquity, so often modified according to the genius and the passions of the legislators who are so numerous in Eastern annals.

If Love was adored as the principle of generation, Mythra was also worshipped for the same reason: and indeed Porphyry calls him Demiurgus, the maker of peoples, the lord of generation.

VOTIVE PHALLI

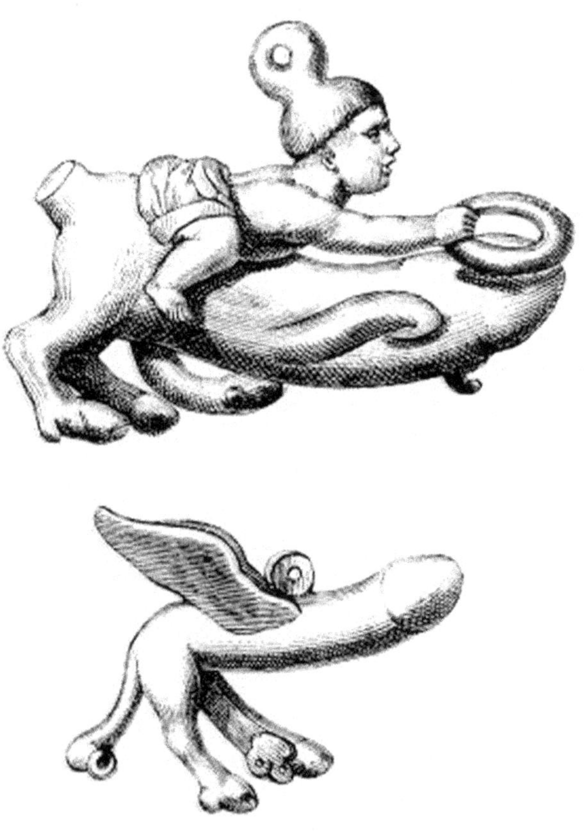

Plate XXV.

A TWO-FOOTED phallus, having itself a second phallus and two wings, or fins, is represented by this lamp. A little child, wearing a kind of Phrygian cap, which served to suspend the lamp, is seated astride on this singular Priapus, and leans to place a crown upon its head. Some antiquaries have considered this crown to be intended as a sort of check which the young rider was desirous to put on his steed; but the opinion does not appear to us tenable. The ancients used bits for their horses which in no wise resembled the object we have here.

This little child astride on a phallus recals the obscene idea which in all times and among all peoples has attached itself to the word ride; in Latin, equitare; in Italian, cavalcare.

The two feet of the animal, which form the body of the lamp, terminate in two heads of phalluses.

From what we have previously said, every reader may explain to himself the meaning of this bronze, for the crown, the feet, the wings, or fins, indicate clearly enough the power of the generative principle innate with all animals living on land, in air, or in water.

Another votive phallus, with wings and the feet of a quadruped.

VOTIVE PHALLI

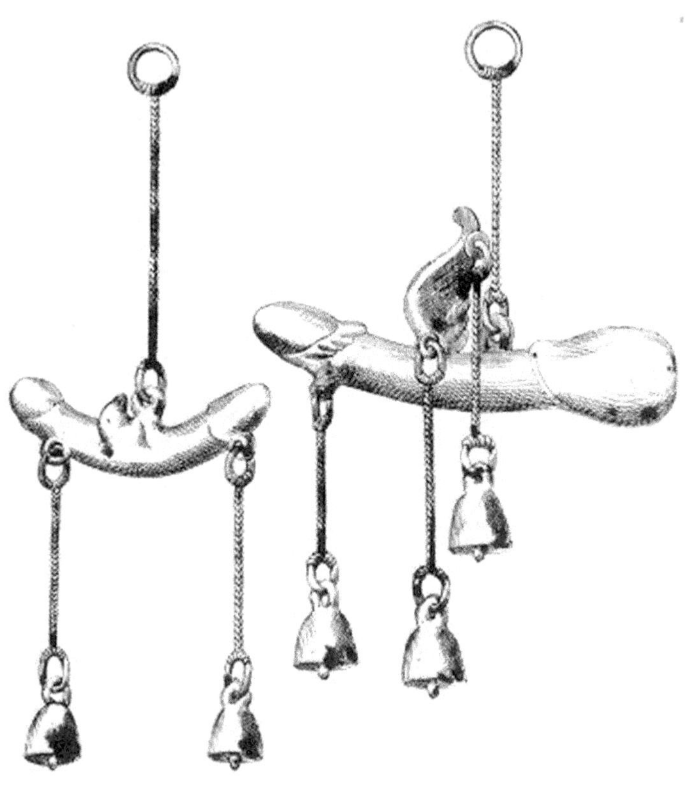

Plate XXVI.

DOUBLE phallus in bronze, with two wings, and two small bells suspended by little chains.

Another phallus in bronze, winged, and ornamented with three small bells.

The interpretation of these bronzes may be sought in what has been already said in relation to the preceding plates or in the Introduction. We will, however, add that, according to Larcher, the phalluses had not always the indecent aspect they here bear. They were sometimes represented in the form of a cross surmounted with a ring, such as is seen on the Isiac Table in the collection of Egyptian Antiquities [1] of Caylus. The triple phallus was also represented by a triple cross surmounted with a ring.

---

[1] Recueil des Antiquites Egyptiennes.

VOTIVE PHALLUS

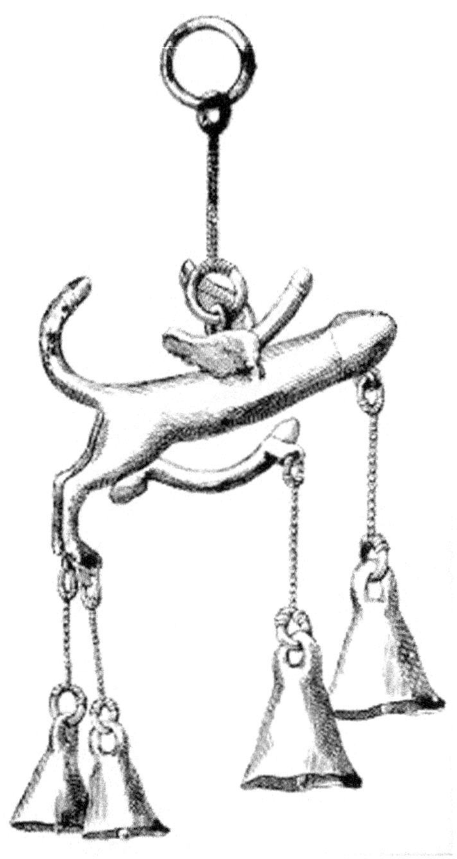

Plate XXVII.

HE hinder part of this bronze is somewhat like a horse. The wings are typical of the rapidity of fecundation. This novel Pegasus has three phalluses, one of which occupies the ordinary place assigned to it by nature among the mammalia. The second is raised like a tail, and the third rises from between the wings, in the place which would be occupied by a rider. It is evident that, from whatever side the maleficent spirit might present itself, it found a talisman ready to repulse it: much in the same way that, in our own day, a public building is surrounded with lightning conductors.

VOTIVE PHALLI

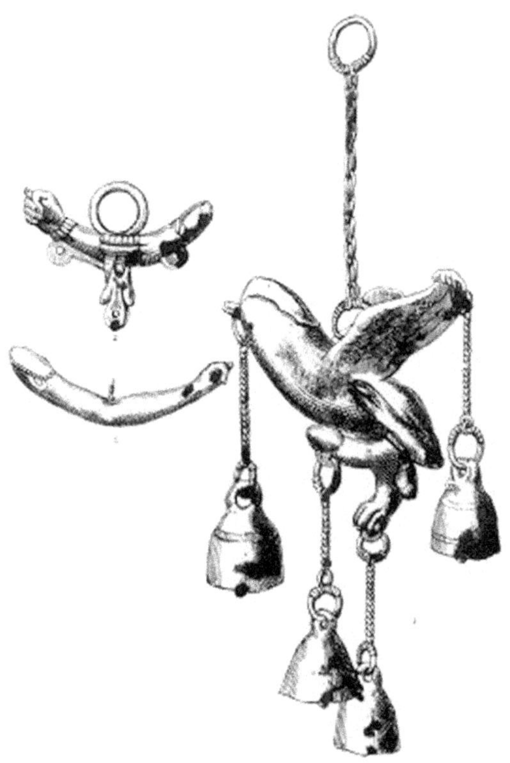

Plate XXVIII.

THE first two figures represent amulets divided into two parts, one of which is in the form of a phallus, and the other of an arm with a hand, making the figue, that obscene gesture which we have spoken of in describing plate 19.

This singular figure, to which are suspended four little bells, in its wings and head resembles a bird, and in the hinder part a lion: a threefold symbol of the generative principle, which fights with the strength of a lion, propagates with the swiftness of an eagle, and triumphs over all obstacles.

> The lion   Strength.
>
> The eagle   Swiftness.
>
> The bells   Triumph.

BRONZE AMULETS

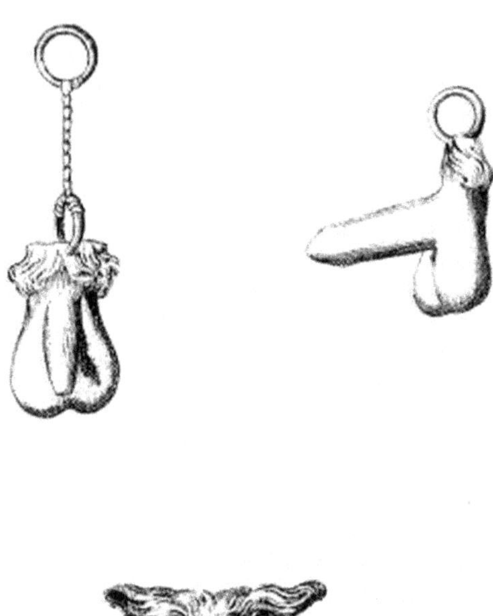

Plate XXIX.

THESE three phalluses in bronze are so many amulets which the ancients were accustomed to wear: the men in order to keep away sorceries, the women for the same object, and also in order that they might become fruitful when they wished. Some of these amulets were made of isinglass, others of bone, ivory, terra cotta, or other material.

Figures 1 and 2 are represented with the rings which were used to suspend them, and No. 3 is perforated with two holes in the form of eyes, through which doubtless a chain was passed.

We have already spoken at sufficient length, both in the Introduction and in the explanation of Plate 7, of the consecration of phalluses, and we have said that the origin of this practice might be traced to the mysteries of Isis; but there exists on this subject another version exceedingly ridiculous and improbable, which nevertheless is dwelt upon very seriously by grave writers, among others, by Clement of Alexandria and Arnobius; but Larcher [1] points out with reason that the Fathers of the Church sometimes allowed themselves to be so far carried away by their zeal for Christianity, or, rather, by their hatred of paganism, as to admit for true absurdities which the heathens themselves would have repudiated.

Clement of Alexandria thus seriously endeavours to show how foul was the origin of the pagan ceremonies Bacchus most ardently desired to descend to Hades, but he was ignorant of the road thither; Prosymnus offered to act as his guide, provided he would accord him a recompense. This recompense would have been dishonourable for any one but Bacchus he was asked to accord to his guide his secret favours.

"Prosymnus having explained himself more clearly, the god promised, on oath, to satisfy him, in case he returned from his expedition. Being guided on the road, he carried out his project; but, on his return, he learnt that Prosymnus was dead. He forthwith proceeded to his tomb to acquit himself of his debt, and there invoked his embraces. Having then broken off the branch of a fig-tree, he cut it into the shape of a phallus, and seating himself upon it, fulfilled to the dead the promise he had made to the living.

"After this event, the phallus was carried in procession through towns in honour of Bacchus, in order to preserve the mystic memory of his deed." [2]

The following is the version of Arnobius:

"When Nysius-Semelcius Liber [1] was still among men, he desired greatly to become acquainted with the infernal regions, and to ascertain what was

---

[1] Larcher, Note 167 on the Second Book of Herodotus.
[2] Clement of Alexandria, Prtrept., page 29.

going on in the realms of Tartarus. But this curiosity of his was attended by some difficulties, seeing that, the journey being an unknown one, he knew not which way to proceed. But a certain Prosumnus, prone enough to improper longings, who had conceived a passion for the god, arose and promised to point out to him the gate of Dis and the entrance to Acherusia, if the god would gratify him, and he might be allowed to take from him uxorious pleasures. The easy god swore by his power and will that it should be done, but not till he had returned from hell, safe and sound. Prosumnus courteously showed the way, and stood on the threshold itself of the infernal regions. In the meantime, while Liber reviewed curiously the lake of Styx, Cerberus, the Furies, and other things, his guide was struck off from the number of the living, and buried according to human fashion. Evyus [2] emerged from the Shades, and finding that his guide was dead, in order that he might fulfil his compact and absolve himself from the obligation of the oath he had sworn, proceeded to his place of burial, and cutting off one of the stoutest branches of a fig-tree, he chipped, stripped, smoothed, and shaped it into form, upon which he fixed it in the earth that covered the tomb, and having stripped himself, sat down on it."

---

[1] Bacchus was surnamed Liber, because wine delivers from all care, and sets the mind at liberty; Nysius, from Nysa, the name of his nurse; Semeleius, from Semele, his mother.

[2] Another surname of Bacchus, derived from Evohe, his war-cry.

THE SURPRISED NYMPH

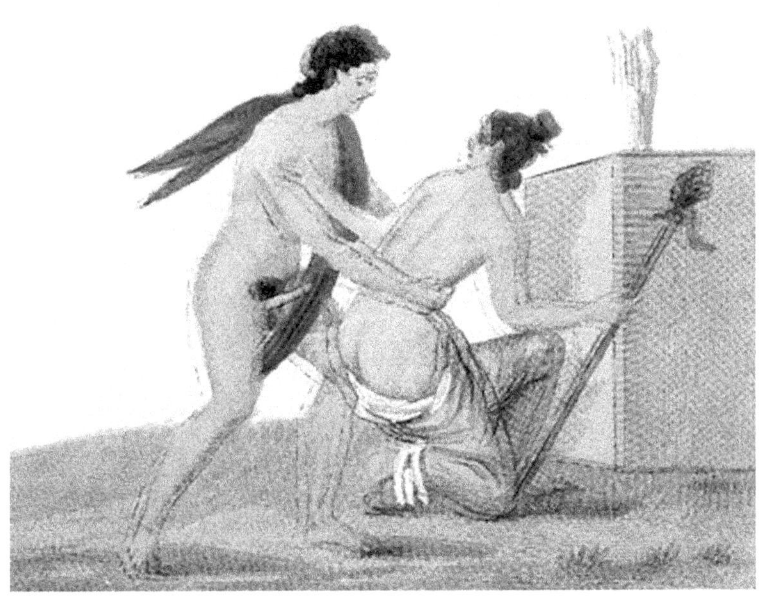

Plate XXX.

A YOUNG girl, bearing a thyrsus, or rather a kind of crook, which would seem to indicate a shepherdess, is sheltering herself at the foot of the statue of Minerva in order to escape from the pursuit of her lover: a symbol of the combats waged by love against wisdom. Her precaution is useless, for the young man, the shape of whose cars would lead us to take him for a faun, tears her away from this last shelter; his ardour, and the weakness with which the young girl repulses him, sufficiently indicate the not far distant issue of the combat.

Some persons have thought that this fresco may represent the rape of Cassandra, committed by Ajax, the son of Oileus, in the temple of Minerva:

"Behold the royal prophetess, the fair
Cassandra, dragg'd by her dishevell'd hair;
Whom not Minerva's shrine, nor sacred bands,
In safety could protect from sacrilegious hands." [1]

This supposition does not seem probable; for the rape of the priestess, the daughter of Priam, often exercised the talent of the artists of antiquity, but never under the form of an allegory. And, indeed, what is the use of allegory in a subject where the painter works with all the licence of art?

The fresco would rather recall an anecdote cited by Apuleius:

"The beautiful Chromis, daughter of the shepherd Chrasias, on going to pray for wisdom in a wood consecrated to Minerva on the eve of her marriage with the young Alcimedes, was surprised by Myrtillus, whose prayers she had disdained, and was sacrificed without pity at the feet of the statue of the goddess. The sacrilegious rival had taken the disguise of a faun. This insult did not go unpunished. Myrtillus never left the sacred wood, and Minerva restored to the young girl her virginity."

However, in this kind of subjects, it often happens that commentators exhaust themselves in conjectures to discover a hidden meaning which did not exist in the mind of the ancients; more especially in the libertine fancies of Greek or Roman artists, it is often useless to look for an allegorical, historical, or imitative idea. Those who painted the frescoes and arabesques in the triclinia and boudoirs of Baïa, Pompeii, and Herculaneum gave themselves up entirely to the folly of their caprice and to the shamelessness common to artists of their time. They only cared to satisfy the passions of the employer, without troubling themselves about the morality of art. It has often happened that an allegory has been understood in a sense opposite to the idea that guided the pencil; thus, in the Nymph Surprised, might we not discover an epigrammatic idea? May it not be a satire against Wisdom, a goddess powerless to save innocence even when it shelters itself at the foot of her altar?

---

[1] VIRG., Æn. II.

Commentators sometimes injure the interests of art when they give forced explanations, and seem to delight in contradictions. It is best to leave a subject of antiquity in that mysterious vagueness which possesses far more charm for the lover of art than that conflict of erudition and science which is neither error nor truth.

THE FLIGHT OF AENEAS

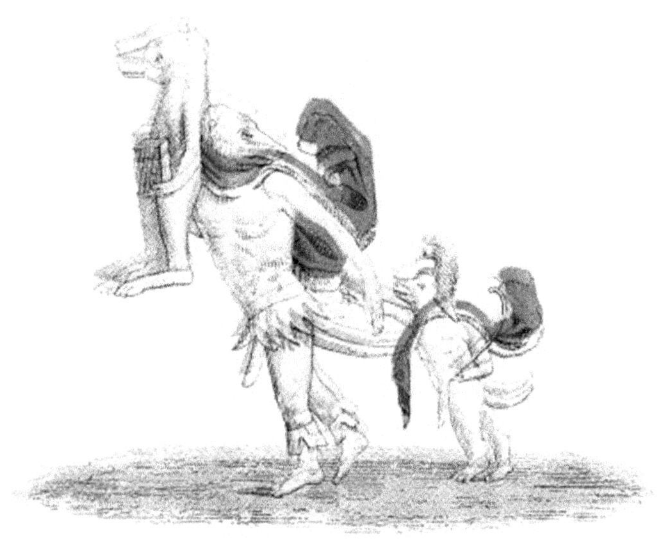

Plate XXXI.

THIS fresco was discovered at Gragnano in 1760, and represents in caricature the flight of Æneas. The ancients were fond of such grotesque representations, which they called cercopitheci (long-tailed monkeys), or cynocephali (dog-headed monkeys). [1]

The Trojan hero wears round his neck that kind of garment which was called a chlamys. It is of dark red, as is also that of young Ascanius. The latter, who wears the Phrygian cap, of the same colour, gives his left hand to his father, and carries in the other a kind of reed or little stick he has picked up while playing on the road; for childhood, happy and heedless,

---

[1] MARTIAL; PLINY; PAUSANIAS.

knows no danger; the features of Anchises, on the other hand, bear the impress of a melancholy gravity. The unfortunate old man has survived the fall of those sacred walls which Hector was unable to protect; but in his flight he has not forgotten his household gods; they are safe in the casket which he holds in his hands. At the same time Æneas, the valiant protector of the family. looks behind, no doubt for his faithful spouse, of whom he is doomed to see nothing more but the plaintive shade. It may easily be seen that the safety of the family had necessarily to depend on him, for he seems to be of a higher organization of life than his companions: he has at least the legs of a man, whereas his father and his son have rather those of a quadruped.

In spite of their dog's heads, these three figures bear the distinctive character of the personages whom they represent. Nor should it be overlooked how carefully the painter has followed the indications of Virgil as they occur in that justly-celebrated second book of the Æneid. The young Ascanius grasps his father's right hand, according to the poet's description

--Dextræ se parvus Iulus
Implicuit. [1]

Too young and feeble to keep up with him, he follows with lagging steps:--
Sequiturque patrem non passibus æquis. [2]
Indeed, in looking at the present fresco, the lines of the poet naturally recur to our memory.

The casket in the hands of Anchises undoubtedly contains the household gods of the family; for the pious Æneas had asked his sire to take care of them, since he was not allowed to touch them, stained as he was with the blood of the battle-field, until he had washed himself in the pure water of a running stream.

"Our country-gods, the relics, and the bands,
Hold you, my father, in your guiltless hands:
In me 'tis impious holy things to bear,
Red as I am with slaughter, new from war:

---

[1] Æn. II.
[2] Ib. II.

Till in some living stream I cleanse the guilt
Of dire debate, and blood in battle spilt."

Finally, the artist has with reason depicted restlessness and even terror in the features of the Trojan hero; for this brave warrior, who did not fear the redoubtable Grecian phalanx, who did not dread their pointed arrows, now takes fright at the least breath of air; the slightest noise makes him tremble, such was his anxiety for the father he carried and the son he led.

"I who so bold and dauntless just before
The Grecian darts and shock of lances bore,
Now take alarm while horrors reign around
At every breeze, and start at every sound."

The reader will see that it would be impossible to carry exactness any farther.

The caricatures of the artists of antiquity were by no means always of so harmless a nature. At Rome it was not unusual for impudent actors to appear on the stage with certain masks bearing the features of the most distinguished citizens of the empire. Such scandals called forth the laughter of the vulgar and the indignation of the well-bred.

Caricature did not therefore originate with modern art. This must be said with pride, because of the great abuse which we have made of this playful weapon, kindly even in its origin, and sometimes grave in its most burlesque features. Castigat ridendo mores.

Perhaps lovers of poetry will not be sorry to see some more of those beautiful lines which follow immediately upon the selection already quoted.

Creusa has lost her way: the pious Æneas, whose heart is sore with the bitterest grief, does not hesitate to retrace his steps in order to seek his faithful companion; he sees once more the palace of Priam and the citadel and temple of Juno

Then with ungoverned madness I proclaim
Through all the silent streets Creusa's name.
Creusa still I call: at length she hears,

And, sudden, thro' the shades of night appears.
Appears no more Creusa, nor my wife,
But a pale spectre, larger than the life.
Aghast, astonish'd, and struck dumb with fear,
I stood; like bristles rose my stiffen'd hair,
Then thus the ghost began to soothe my grief:
'Nor tears, nor cries, can give the dead relief;
Desist, my much-loved lord, to indulge your pain
You bear no more than what the gods ordain.
My fates permit me not from hence to fly;
Nor he, the great comptroller of the sky.
Long wandering ways for you the powers decree
On land hard labours and a length of sea.
Then, after many painful years are past,
On Latium's happy shore you shall be cast
Where gentle Tiber from his bed beholds
The flowery meadows and the feeding folds.
There end your toils; and there your fates provide
A quiet kingdom, and a royal bride:
There fortune shall the Trojan line restore
And you for lost Creusa weep no more.
Fear not that I shall watch with servile shame
The imperious looks of some proud Grecian dame:
Or, stooping to the victor's lust, disgrace
My goddess-mother, or my royal race.
And now farewell: the parent of the gods
Restrains my fleeting soul in her abodes:
I trust our common issue to your care,'
She said; and, gliding, pass'd unseen in air.
I strove to speak, but horror tied my tongue,
And thrice about her neck my arms I flung:
And, thrice deceived, on vain embraces hung.
Light as an empty dream at break of day,
Or as a blast of wind, she rush'd away." [1]

---

[1] ÆN. II., Dryden's translation.

THE FAUN'S KISS

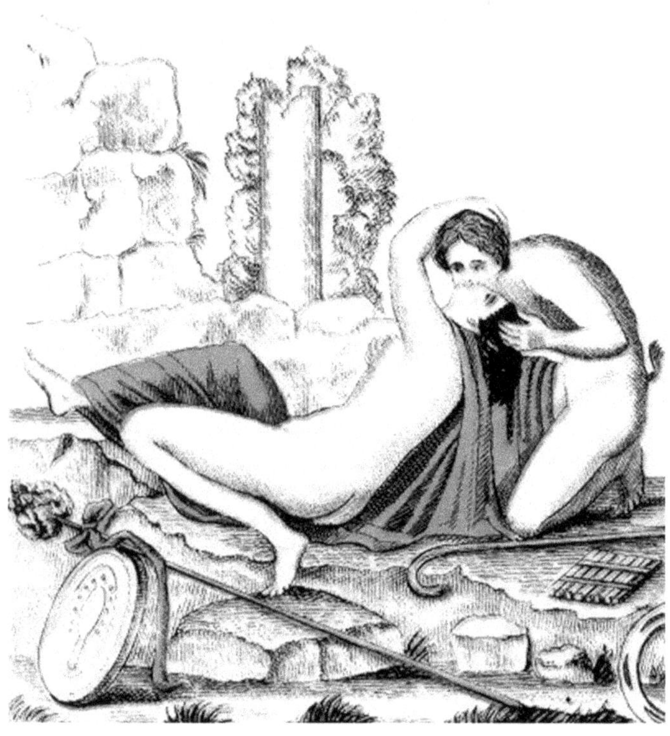

Plate XXXII.

THE objects of art discovered in the excavations of Herculaneum are, as a rule, far superior in execution to those found at Pompeii. The delightful painting, reproduced faithfully in our plate, has already been given, but very imperfectly, by the academicians of Naples, by David, in the work of Sylvan Maréchal, and by Piroli.

What a mingled expression of daring and desire is there in the Faun, who has rushed unawares upon a Bacchant imprudently traversing a solitary and secret place. He has flung her down; his mouth has met that of the nymph, and his hand is stealing over her voluptuous bosom. The beautiful Bacchant, however, far from showing anger at this excess of boldness, displays in every movement of her body a burning intoxication, an impatient lust which chides his delay, and summons him to proceed to closer endearments.

At the feet of the two lovers we may see the pastoral crook (pedum), the seven-reeded flute [1] (syrinx), the rattle-drum (tympanum) on which is Painted a cistrum, the thyrsus, and a cercle sans fond.

The colouring of this fresco is as brilliant as the design is graceful. The flesh-tint of the two wrestlers differs in, tone just as they differ in sex. Cinnabar has been lavished on the Bacchant's mantle and on the riband of her thyrsus. We recognise in her a nymph of coquettish manners; and the artist has taken care to omit no detail to make us envy the young Faun's good fortune as we look upon her.

The celebrated Canova has imitated this very graceful group in one of his charming compositions.

---

[1] The present example has eight; but this was probably an oversight of the painter, to whom we are indebted for this delicious fresco.

A SATYR AND A BACCHANTE

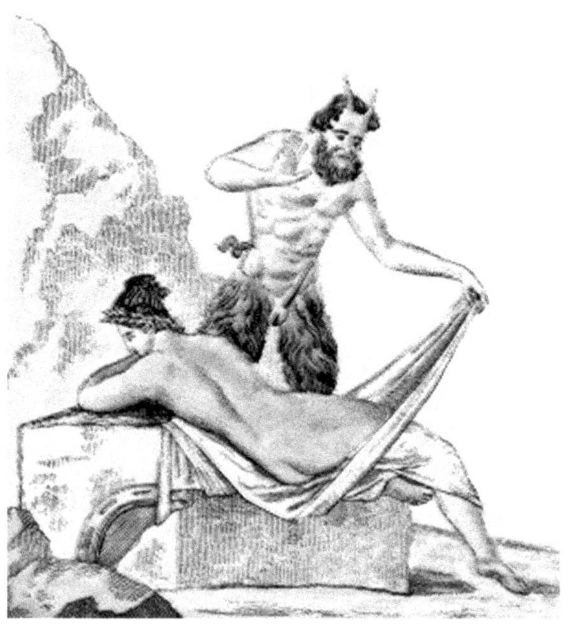

Plate XXXIII.

A BACCHANT crowned with ivy has chosen a solitary place to rest herself; but the tambour which we see near her seems to indicate that she wished her retreat to be no secret mystery to the inhabitants of these solitudes. She reclines voluptuously; her beautiful head is artfully turned aside; but her half-shut eyes show that she only feigns to be asleep in order the better to favour the attempts of which she is about to be the object. And indeed one satyr, attracted no doubt by the sound of the music, approaches, and, judging by the apparent slumber of the nymph that the moment is favourable, boldly lifts up the veil which covered her beauty. His lascivious looks, his gaping nostrils, his attitude and gestures, all indicate admiration and desire.

VENUS ON HER SHELL CONCH

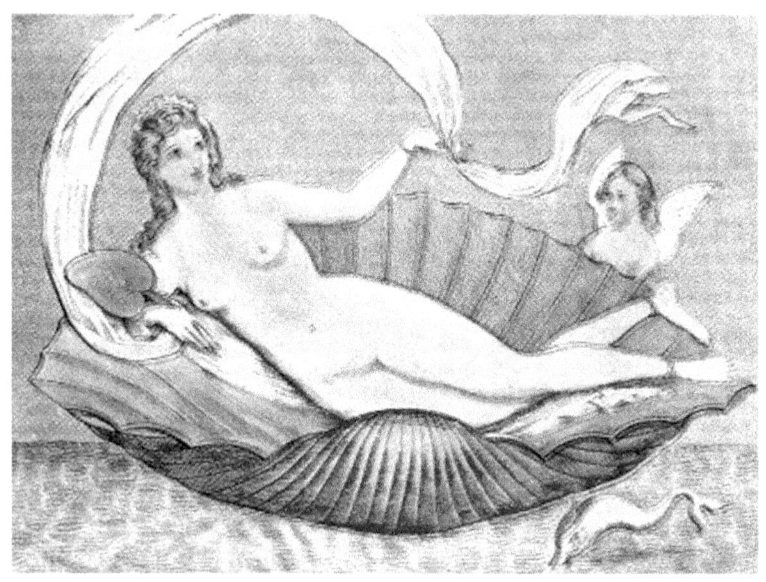

Plate XXXIV.

THIS graceful painting would not have dishonoured the pencil of Titian. The Queen of Love is reclining on a sea-shell; Cupid and a dolphin are her attendants. A pure and limpid stream cradles her softly on its surface, and her scarf, swollen by the breath of the zephyrs, serves as a sail for the frail bark.

The form of the goddess is equally noble and voluptuous; her beautiful hair, surmounted by an elegant diadem, falls in wavy curls over her alabaster shoulders.

We feel that such beauty cannot be the portion of any mortal. She wears bracelets on her arms and feet; in her right hand we observe a leaf of lily.

Roman ladies made use of the leaf of the lily (nymphæ) after the manner of a fan.

The dolphin was consecrated to Venus. Several mythologists have erroneously represented this as a fabulous fish. There is nothing fabulous about it except the form that painters attribute to it. It has been said that this fish was consecrated to Venus on account of her penchant for young girls, and this ridiculous explanation has been seriously reproduced by the academicians of Herculaneum and by Sylvain Maréchal, following them. The dolphin generally swims on the surface of the waters; we have ourselves seen numerous troops of them at the entrance of the gulf of Naples, between the island of Capri and Cape Misena. Its movements resemble those of a little boat, which rises and falls again with the wave that carries it.

This charming fresco was found at Gragnano in 1762. It served as the perspective to a small garden.

SPINTHRIA

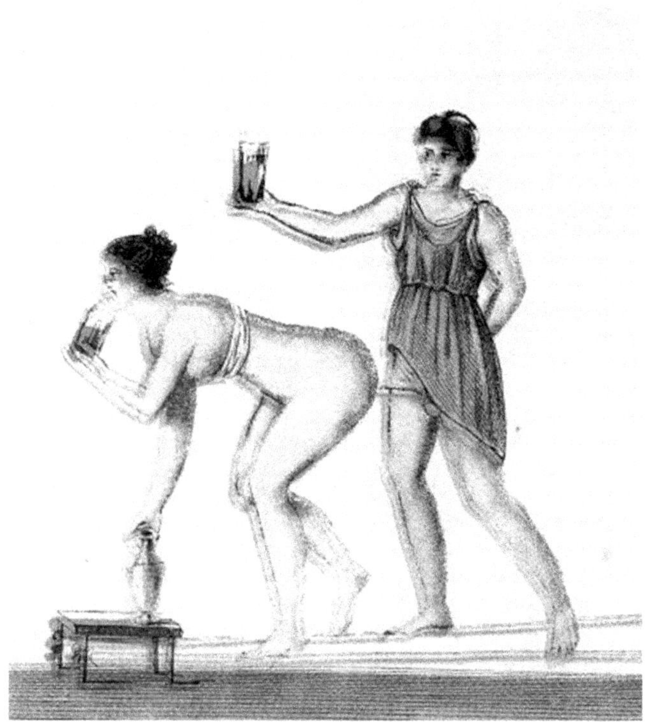

Plate XXXV.

TWO rope-dancers, a man and a woman, are indulging themselves while in a state of perfect equilibrium. In this singular painting we have before us one of those scenes of orgy which were the delight of Nero and Tiberius. The actors in it, placed on two out-stretched ropes, caress each other without losing their equilibrium, and drink without spilling a drop of the liquor contained in their glasses.

This fresco, remarkable for its purity of design and brilliant colouring, is obscene to a degree. It appears indeed that, if the hero of the occasion has not lost his balance, he has at least lost his way, and gone completely astray. In a word, such is the position of these ardent acrobats that we cannot do otherwise than conclude that the artist supposed the chief actor intended to claim from his fair companion that shameful favour which Martial could not obtain from his wife, but which, if he may be believed, discreet matrons accorded to their husbands:--

Sweet heart, begone, or use our ways with us,
I am no Curius, Numa, Tatius.
Nights spent in pleasant cups best please my sense,
Thou to drink water canst rise and dispense.
Thou joy'st in darkness, I by light to sport,
Or else by day to loose my breeches for 't.
Swathes or coats cover thee, or obscure stuff,
No wench to me can lie display'd enough,
Such kisses please like doves that are a-billing,
Thou smack'st me like thy granddam, so unwilling,
Nor towards the work dost voice or motion bring,
Nor hand, but makest it as some offering.
The Phrygian boys in secret spent their seed
As oft as Hector's wife rid on his steed.
Whilst her lord slept, Penelope, though chaste,
Was wont to play her hand below her waist.
Thou'll not be ------, although Gracchus' wife,
Pompey's and others did it without strife.
And when the boy not present was,
It is said, To fill wine, Juno was Jove's Ganymede.
If gravity by day doth thee delight,
Lucretia be; I'll have thee Lais by night." [1]

The vice, of which this fresco seems to be a representation, has been perpetuated openly enough, in warm countries, to the present day. We must not be understood to speak of the disgusting caresses of two persons of the same sex, but of the kind of union Cornelia accorded to Gracchus, Julia to Pompey, and Portia to Brutus.

---

[1] MARTIAL, xi. 105. R. Fletcher's Translation, 1656.

If the men of the South may be credited, their wives do not always look upon this connection merely as an act of complaisance on their part. This singular custom must, perhaps, be accounted for by the influence of the climate, which inspires such quick and burning desires that it appears at first sight impossible to extinguish them by the vulgar and ordinary methods of enjoyment; and in seeking to refine their pleasure, they deprave

it, The same influence also acts on the physical organization of Southern women; their favours offer such material facilities, that it might be feared disgust would succeed to love without the stimulants capable of re-awakening the ardours of the latter. And, finally, such faults might be accounted for with regard to certain women by the fear they have of the consequences of their weakness when they act imprudently with men. An eloquent writer on Love [1] thus speaks on this subject: "Such a departure from propriety in women would excite little indignation if prudence alone could render a departure from propriety lawful. They are desirous, it might be said, of escaping from the disquietude and from all the dangers of a more natural union. Ought the sex which does not pardon them to disguise from itself that they have too good reason to fear what they would doubtless have chosen, and that too often that which they must necessarily always prefer becomes fatal to them. Let us not be eager to judge them; and, without justifying them, let us admit that they may daily be placed in embarrassing situations, and that such difficulties extenuate many faults."

---

[1] M. de Senancour.

MERCURY AND YPHTIMA

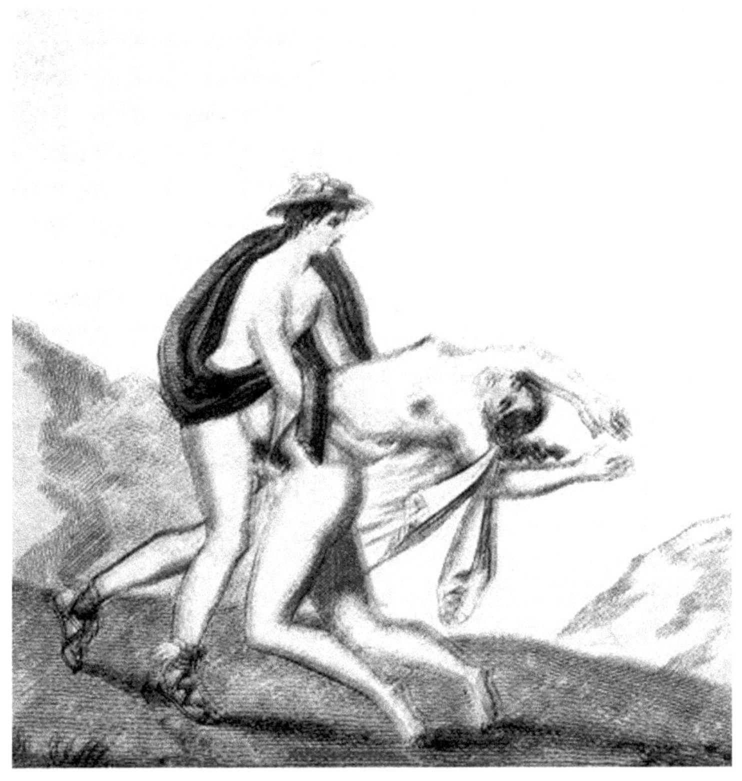

Plate XXXVI.

YPHTIMA, the nymph, had offended the gods; Mercury, being commissioned to conduct her to Hades, led her to a solitary place and ravished her. Such appears to be the subject of this painting. The drawing is incorrect and in bad taste, while the exaggerated positions are quite devoid of probability.

From this union of Mercury and Yphtima arose the satyrs.

At Cyllene, in Elidia, there was a temple where Mercury was worshipped. The god was represented there in a most indecent posture, symbolical of fecundity. Wit and eloquence were the attributes of Mercury, and it was natural that the ancients should revere in him those powerful auxiliaries of seduction and pleasure. [1]

---

[1] PAUSANIAS.

AN EROTIC SCENE

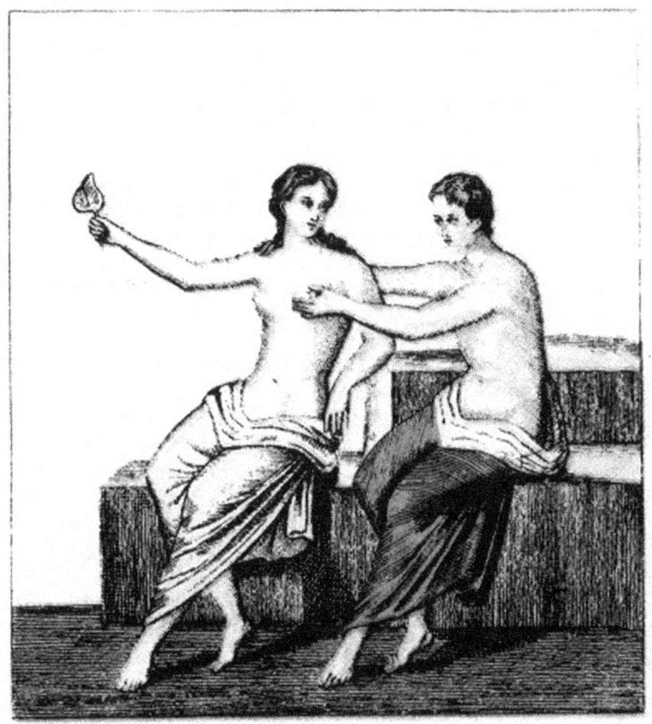

Plate XXXVII.

A YOUNG woman, half-naked, is showing her lover a quince-tree leaf, as if to excite him to take what she still refuses him. The youth amorously presses his mistress's neck and shoulders, and looks anxiously at the leaf which the latter holds in her hand, and which doubtless the painter considered as the symbol of a virginity ready to be plucked.

It was the custom at Rome to give the bride a quince to eat before conducting her to the nuptial bed. We may therefore consider this fresco as a representation of the first private intercourse between a young married pair.

The figures are perfectly well preserved; but the same thing cannot be said of the background of the fresco. In its present state, the actors look as if they were seated on banks of stone; but we are inclined to think they were originally seen seated on cushions, in a chamber covered with drapery. The youth's legs are concealed by a red mantle, and those of the young woman by the flammeum, a garment of gold-coloured silk, set apart for brides. Still, in order completely to set aside all doubt as to the subject of this plate, the girdle or belt is wanting which Roman virgins left their husbands to untie on the bridal night.

The flower, leaf, and fruit of the quince-tree were all dedicated by the Greeks to the phallus, and by the Indians to the lingam.

We are indebted to the learned German historian Niebuhr for some valuable details as to the manner in which marriage was celebrated among the Romans.

The first solemnity was the confarreation. It took place in the presence of ten witnesses, and with the intervention of the pontiffs. The farreum, or sacred cake, was offered to the betrothed pair; five torches were lighted in their presence; the betrothed woman touched water and fire, and performed other ceremonies equally symbolical. After this solemnity, the woman was in the hands and power of the man who had become her husband: she took his name, and became his presumptive heiress, concurrently with her children.

This ceremony did not take place for free marriage, a sort of union which did not confer on the wife the name of her husband or the right of inheritance, and which, on the other hand, gave him no power over her. These are what are still called in Germany left-handed marriages.

A woman who came under the absolute power of her husband might be condemned by him to the penalty of death for certain offences more or less grave, among which may be remarked that of drinking wine. The use of this beverage was generally forbidden to women, under the severest penalties: this was a law of the Twelve Tables.

But a woman was not under her husband's power until they had passed a year together beneath the conjugal roof, and she could break through the prescription by absenting herself every year for three nights.

After the betrothal, the man gave his future mate a metal ring and a kiss. On the appointed day, the relations and friends of the married pair conducted them to the temple with great pomp; the procession was led by young children who carried a work-basket, a distaff it torch, and a branch of hawthorn. joyous cries might be heard, among which that of Thalossio, was distinguished; instrumental players joined the procession, and accompanied it as far as the temple. There the pontiffs celebrated the union after consulting the auspices.

Then the young wife was conducted with the same pomp to her husband's abode. On reaching the threshold of the door, she sprinkled it with an odoriferous oil, and her companions immediately seized her and lifted her across the threshold in their arms. Then came, as in our own day, the famous marriage-feast, so coveted by all the guests, and so tedious for the newly-married pair, the cynosure of every eye, and the mark for every stale and worn-out jest,

Finally, the young wife, clad, as we have said, in the flammeum, crowned with lemon-flower, and, above all, adorned with the precious virginal zone, was led by her relations and companions to the conjugal chamber, where it quince was given her to eat, and every one immediately retired, leaving her alone with her husband and the cubicular slave. The latter also withdrew, after bringing his mistress's shoes, carefully shut up in a precious casket, and placed himself as a sentinel behind the door, attentively watching that no inquisitive intruder came to disturb the mysteries of the nuptial bed.

SPINTHRIA

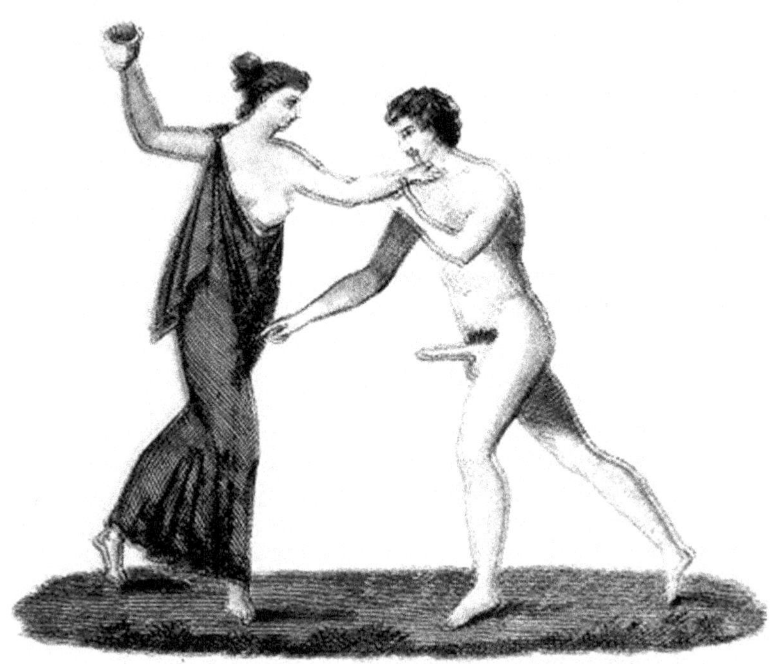

Plate XXXVIII.

THIS fresco was discovered in 1826, at Pompeii. It is supposed that the house where it was found was one of those places of debau-chery called lupanaria. In one of the principal rooms of the house may be seen a painting representing some youths and courtezans abandoning to the pleasures of the table and to play: one of the young men, the hero of the fresco we are describing, heated, doubtless, by the fumes of wine, is pursuing a woman. His gestures leave no doubt as to the nature of his intentions; but his fair companion, alarmed at the sight of the prodigious instrument with which he menaces her, seizes her lover by the throat, and endeavours to push him back: she even seems on the point of hurling at his head a vase which she holds in her right hand.

The drawing of this fresco presents several imperfections, and the youth's left arm, though meant to be foreshortened, is evidently not long enough.

We mentioned in our Introduction that the Greeks called these sort of paintings grylli, and the Romans libidines. They were designated by a more emphatic expression when they were more than usually indecorous, viz., Spinthria (debauchery), from σπινθὴρ, a spark. We shall henceforth make use of this term, as more appropriate to the paintings which remain to be described.

SPINTHRIA

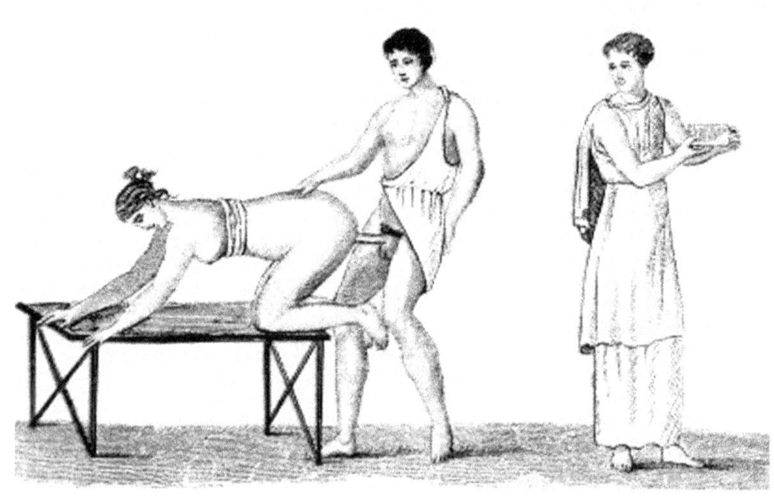

Plate XXXIX.

THIS erotic painting undoubtedly represents a bridal night. The young bride still wears her virgin's zone, and, according to the custom of the period, the husband will have to remove it after the consummation of the first sacrifice. The cubicular slave, who may be perceived in the, distance, carries a casket of essences and perfumes. The two young people have chosen the attitude they deemed most suitable to facilitate the accomplishment of the act to which they are proceeding, more ferarum. Finally, the words lente inpelle, which may be read at the bottom of the picture, further demonstrate that the actress in this scene is a young woman who has pardon for her inexperience. "Push gently, spare me!" delightful words you will not long resound in the ears of the conqueror! The proud rider will soon require the spur.

The position adopted by our two personages is often enough found graven stones and Etruscan vases, which is not at all surprising, for it seems: to us that Voltaire made a doubly bad joke when he put into the mouth of Dorothea the singular reproach which she addresses to Joan of Arc

"But I avow I can't conceive
How one goes through the preparation
Needed in such a situation."

This attitude seems dictated by nature itself, and it is certain that in the beginning of societies men who desired to have intercourse with their wives, not having the means of throwing them down on a bed of down at the end of a mysterious alcove, would not have dreamt of stretching them on stones. The attitude which the quadrupeds taught them must have seemed the most commodious and natural.

Plutarch says: "It is thus known that the Delphians are not wanting in what they call Venus-Harma, that is to say, the yoked chariot, nor Homer, when he calls such a conjunction φιλὸτης, which is to say, friendship," &c.

For the rest, the conformation and position of the organs of generation in both sexes sufficiently point out that the work may be accomplished in this way with the best advantage to the reproduction of the human species. Let us hear what Lucretius says on this subject:--

"The sage who views minute
Herds, and the savage tribes by nature led,
Holds that the virtuous matron chief conceives,
When, with subsiding chest and loins erect,
Her dulcet charms she offers, fittest then
The luscious tide to absorb; for nought avail
Exerted motions, the perpetual heave
Of frame high-strain'd and ever-labouring lungs.
These, rather, urged beneath the tender fray,
All fruit prohibit; since the genial share
Oft turn they from the furrow as it holds
Its course direct, and break the impinging shock.' [1]

---

[1] DE RERUM NATURA, iv. Dr. Mason Good's Translation.

This fresco has been recently discovered. The drawing is not very correct: it may especially be remarked that the arms of the principal actor are out of all proportion to the other parts of his body.

AN HERMAPHRODITE

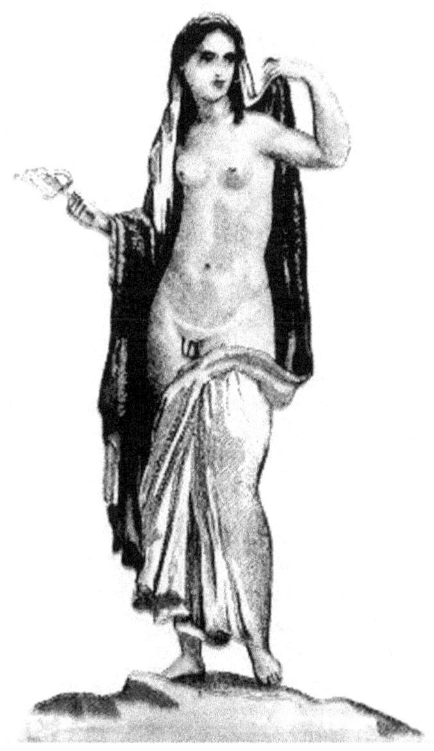

Plate XL.

THIS figure represents an hermaphrodite full of grace, youth, and beauty. We have given some particulars respecting these fabulous beings in the Introduction to this work; and we have also explained why the leaf of the water-lily was consecrated to them.

The hermaphrodite here represented gracefully raises the mantle in which he is enveloped, and reveals at one and the same time the organ of virility and a woman's breast.

An attentive examination of this painting will show that such a being could not exist. The beauty which glows in every one of his limbs; the softness revealed by the rounded forms; everything, in this figure, betrays a sensible and passive being, created for resistance and defeat; there is nothing there, on the other hand, to indicate the vigour and boldness of character which is the birthright of the sex made to attack and to conquer.

This fresco was among the excavations of Pompeii.

AN HERMAPHRODITE AND FAUN

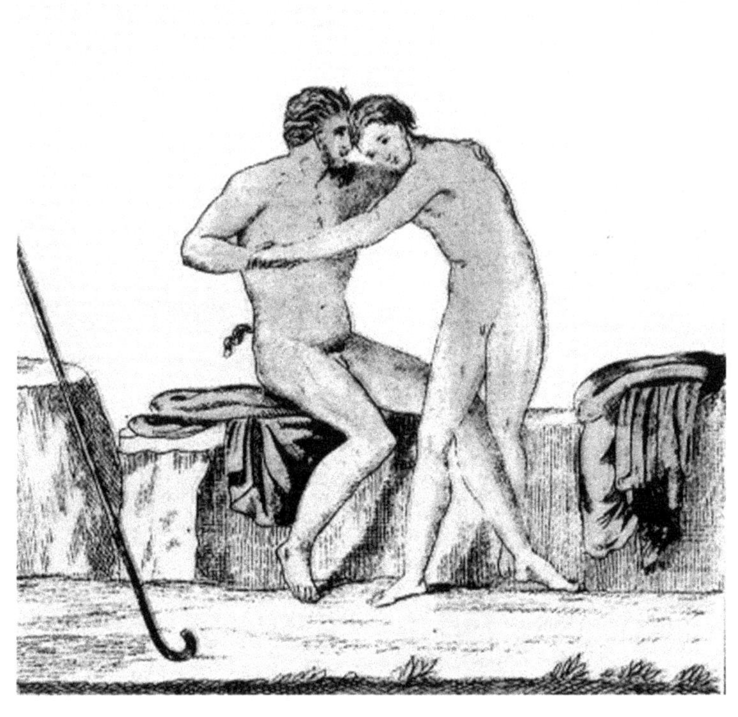

Plate XLI.

THIS charming fresco, excellent in colour and of very remarkable purity of drawing, represents one of those bearded fauns called Sileni, who is trying to do violence to a young hermaphrodite. The place is solitary and rocky; near the Silenus we observe the bent crook, or pedum. The two actors are entirely naked.

This painting is evidently allegorical. The old Silenus, seated on a rock, and seeking to enjoy a being who unites in himself the two senses, is the emblem of those old men, given up to debauchery, who endeavour to reanimate their deadened passions by excess and variety of enjoyment.

The taste of some old men for both sexes is a consequence of the impotency of their resources; they would fain rekindle, by the refinement and monstrosity of their pleasures, a spark of the sacred fire which animates Youth. Such, we think, was the idea which guided the capricious pencil of the author of this fresco.

A SATYR AND HERMAPHRODITE

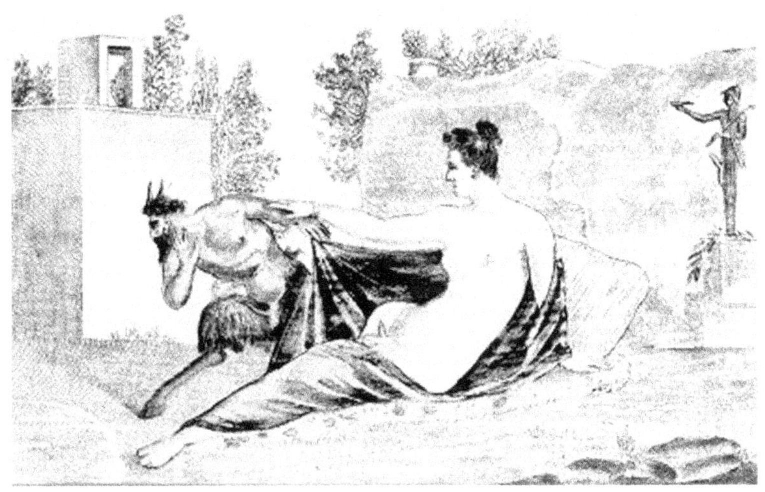

Plate XLII.

A SATYR has surprised a nymph asleep in a solitary place. He prepares to violate her, and already having lifted up the veil that envelops her, he casts a profane look on her most secret charms; but imagine his confusion on perceiving that he has accosted a hermaphrodite! Full of shame and vexation, he seeks to fly; but the hermaphrodite, whose sleep was doubtless only a feint, tries to hold him, and seems himself to promise him pleasures of which he had not dreamt.

In order that nothing may be wanting to complete the obscenity of this painting, we observe in the background a Hermes, crowned with the petasus, bearing in one hand the pedum, or pastoral crook, and in the other the drinking-vessel, in the shape of a horn, called κρατὴρ.

As we have already remarked, these Hermes, with gigantic phalluses, were placed at the entrance of gardens to keep away robbers and sorcerers.

They generally bore an inscription the idea of which was as pleasant as the expression was unseemly. We will quote two, taken at random from the collection entitled Priapeia:

Fœmina si furtum faciet mihi virque puerque,
Hæc cunnum, caput hic, præbeat ille nates.

Pr. Carm., xxi.

Quod sim ligneus, ut vides, Priapus,
Et falx lignea, ligneusque penis:
Prendam te tamen et tenebo prensam:
Totamque hanc sine fraude, quantacumque est,
Tormento, citharaque tensiorem,
Ad costam tibi septimam recondam.

Pr. Carm., cv.

This fresco is not without merit, and the outlines are soft and well drawn, the poses agreeable, and the figures rich in expression; but the Satyr is evidently too short, and the painter has misunderstood the laws of perspective. The contact of the two persons who form both foreground and background makes this disparity still more noticeable.

The hermaphrodite is reclining on a leopard's skin; his mantle is of a beautiful sky-blue colour, and behind him may be perceived an elegant cushion. The colouring of this fresco is truly wonderful considering its great age.

A FAUN AND BACCHANTE

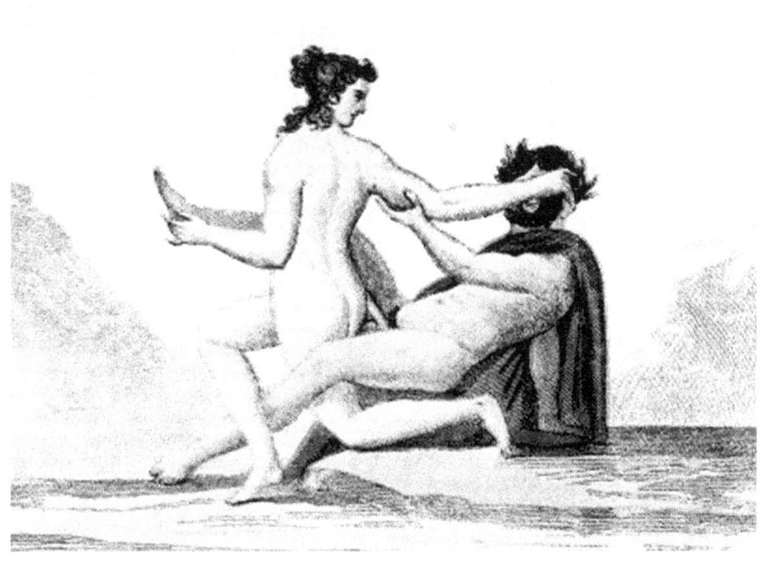

Plate XLIII.

A FAUN is engaged in contest with a nymph. The originality of the poses is not less remarkable than the purity of the drawing.

An amorous encounter has sprung up between the god and the nymph: the former slips and falls, but it does not appear his fair companion desires seriously to take advantage of this accident in order to escape the fate which awaits her. It Is evident that she defends herself feebly: her features, her inflamed look, her nakedness, all betray that she is willing to be vanquished. She knows that her own defeat will furnish her with new arms to subjugate and enchain the happy conqueror in his turn.

In the background of this fresco is a very simple landscape, not well preserved.

SPINTHRIA

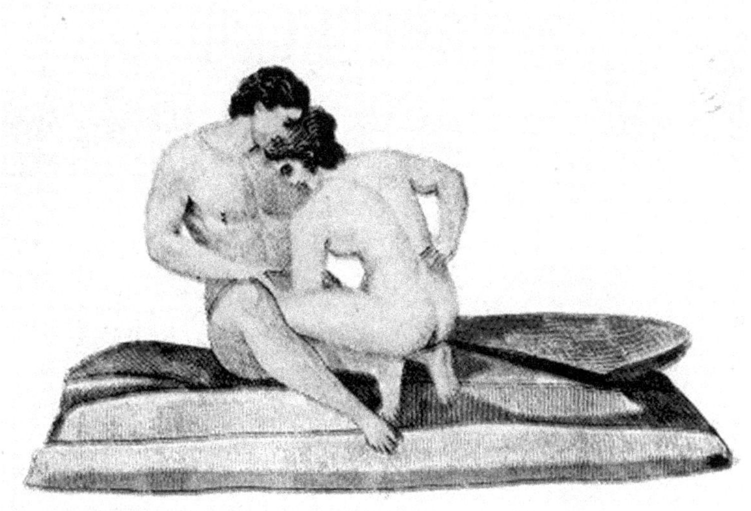

Plate XLIV.

THIS fresco, found at Pompeii, is unquestionably, as regards merit of execution, one of the most remarkable of them all. We stated in our Introduction that obscene paintings entered at Rome into the domain of second-rate painters; but, making allowance for the decline of the art, it cannot be doubted that the author of this fresco must have been a very skilful artist for his time. Contrary to usage, we here find some expression in the features of the two actors: their attitude has nothing trivial; it has that natural character stripped of dignity which strikes and humiliates us, even at the moment when our imagination is fascinated by amorous desires. As is usual with natives of the South, the flesh-tints of the hero of this scene are of a very decided brown. The right arm of the woman, resting on her haunch, doubtless leaves something to be desired;

but it is a foreshortening--a rock against which more than one modern painter has split.

A mere glance at this plate suffices us to guess the subject of it; and indeed it would be rather difficult to explain it in sober language.

SPINTHRIA

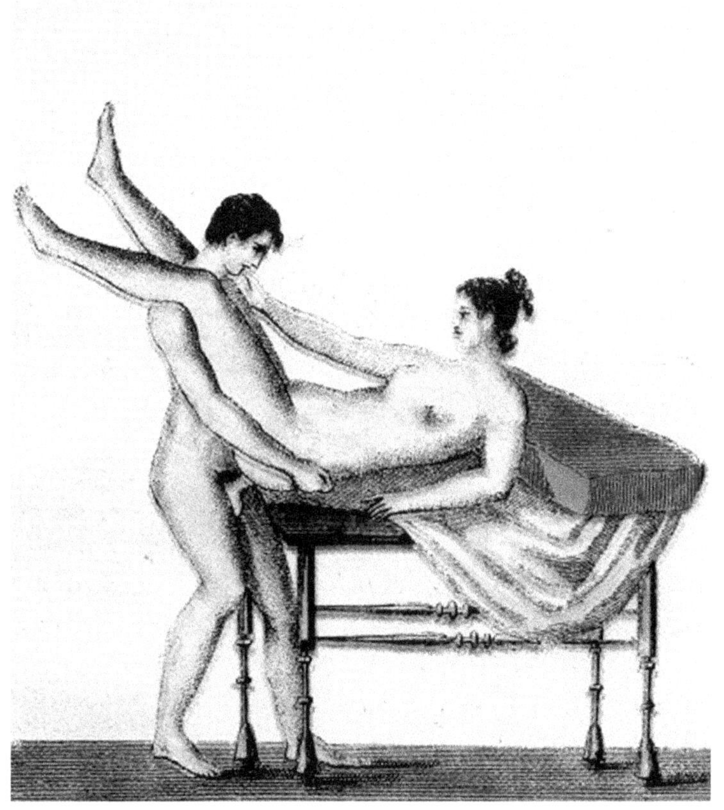

Plate XLV.

HERE again we have an obscene painting, which recalls to mind a species of libertinism much in vogue at Rome in the reigns of the Emperors. The most undeniable antiquities, the authorities most worthy of belief, all concur in demonstrating to us that unnatural enjoyment was tolerated at this period by Roman manners, just as it had been before by Greek manners. We have already said that Virgil, Martial, Persius, Juvenal, Petronius, and other writers, who were read everywhere, and whose productions were admired publicly, celebrated these extravagant unions.

However clumsy and inexpert we may suppose the painter to be to whom we owe the fresco opposite, we cannot doubt that his intention was to represent a lover obtaining from his mistress the favours to which Sodom has attached an immortal name. To convince ourselves of this, it suffices to examine how far the young athlete has lifted his obliging companion on his shoulders. They are both naked, appear young and beautiful, and are reclining on a bed of gilded bronze.

Although this shameful weakness arose in southern climates, where public manners still secretly tolerate it, unnatural enjoyment is certainly far from being unknown in more northern latitudes, but there it is the object of more direct punishment. In England, when the act has been committed with a person of the male sex, it is punished with death:--a barbarous law which is all the more to be deplored, because it really tends to palliate the offender's guilt, bringing down on him as it does the public commiseration by reason of the exaggerated punishment. We must not allow the horror which a bad action inspires in us to drive us to vengeance which inspires equal horror in others. In the same country seduction and adultery art visited with a much lighter punishment; and we conceive this to be a gross absurdity. For, in the first case, that in which the pain of death is carried out, society receives a far less injury, since it affects only the accomplices of it, and cannot have results which fall to the public charge. Nor is it a case for stretching to their extreme latitude the protection which the law owes to the weak against the strong; as the force of resistance may generally, both morally and physically, be adequately proportioned to the force of attack.

Man is not born essentially perverse; he enters into society good by nature; but bad laws create bad morals. Every time the weight of punishment surpasses the enormity of the crime committed, the law falls into disrespect, and consequently into desuetude; and thus people draw the conclusion that the offence formerly condemned has become lawful. At Rome, a law of the Twelve Tables authorized the husband to destroy his wife when the latter was convicted of having drunk wine or committed adultery. The very identity of punishment for two actions so widely dissimilar and different in degrees of turpitude was itself a monstrosity. The legislator, indeed, conceived that, as wine deprives the person using it of the use of reason, it might lead to the most guilty excesses; but, according to this principle, justice would have required that the use of the beverage should be prohibited equally to both sexes. It is no argument to say that men have stronger heads and more solid reason, for in the very countries where wine is accessible to everybody, for one woman, ten men may be seen in a state of drunkenness. The law we have alluded to soon fell into desuetude, as might have been foreseen; husbands allowed their wives the use of wine; and as for adultery, it acquired the freedom of the city at Rome, in spite of the law; so that even the good Cato thought it no dishonour and no extraordinary thing to lend his wife to one of his friends. Ovid addressed a copy of verses to the husband of one of his mistresses, begging him to be a little more jealous in future, as his indifference on this matter deprived the poet of that sense of fear and danger which add so much sweetness to love.

As we have already said, Roman manners authorized the kind of libertinism which appears to be represented on our plate:

"What would you do?" said I, "do you forget that I am a young woman, and not a boy?"

"You have the courage, then," he replied, "to refuse us the favour never denied us yet by any of the women of Rome, most illustrious for their wit and beauty, you who are not less beautiful and witty than the best!"

"But I have a horror of the action," I rejoined, "which I cannot get rid of; you are going to engage in a warfare with me to which I am quite unaccustomed."

"It will not be your death," he said, laughingly. "Much younger women than you have made themselves famous among us by putting their body to a similar use. The loss of your virginity formerly cost you very dear." [1]

---

[1] JOANNIS MEURSII. Elegantia Latini Sermonis.

SPINTHRIA

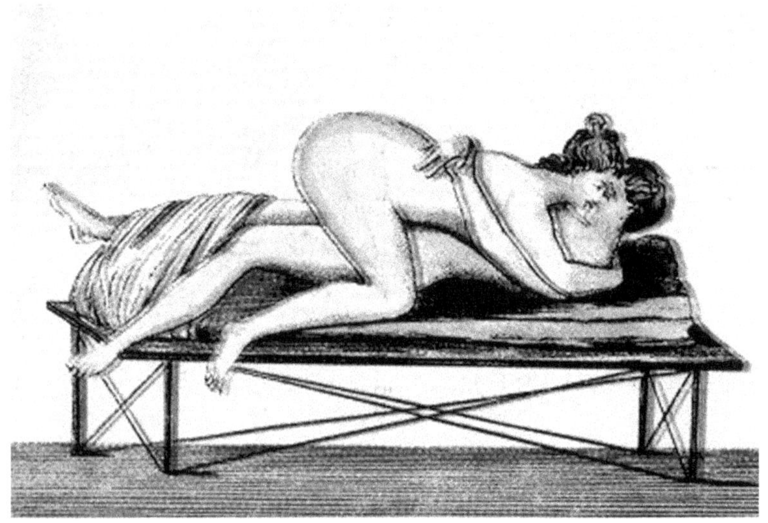

Plate XLVI.

IT must be admitted, this highly obscene painting would not be unworthy of the infamous collections of Aretine. None of the supposed refinements of pleasure were unknown to the ancients. Here, for instance, may be seen two amorous athletes who have changed places in the combat of Venus. Their youth seems emasculated, as it requires a new spur. The sex whom nature has destined to make the attack, and for whom she reserves the conqueror's crown, submits on this occasion to pass for vanquished. The youth is reclining languidly on a heavy mattress, and submits to the whole weight of a feeble woman, who is stript both of her vestments and of the still less transparent veil of modesty.

Of all the extravagances to which the delirium of a lustful imagination may lead, there could perhaps hardly be any less excusable in the two accomplices. For the man misconceives the nobleness of his character and the dignity of his nature, and the woman forgets that, of all her attractions, there is none more seductive than that amiable weakness which allows her to succumb while still resisting.

This painting was discovered not very long ago, at Pompeii. The drawing, as in most of the other Spinthriæ, is not very correct. The bed is formed of a sort of table, the four legs of which seem to be fixed by the help of cords crossing and recrossing each other.

SPINTHRIA

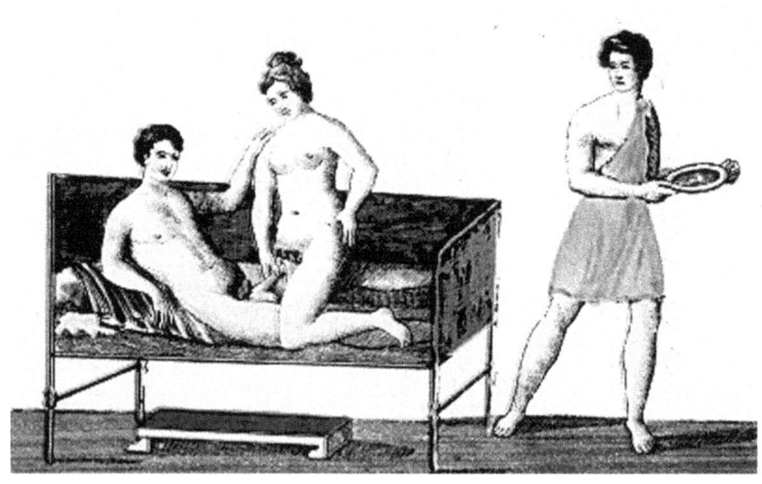

Plate XLVII.

THIS painting is almost a repetition of the preceding one. A young girl, seated astride over her lover, is again playing the chief part. The cubicular slave, on the point of withdrawing from the mysterious chamber, turns round and casts a lascivious look on the two lovers. He bears a dish, upon which nothing is seen, and which probably contained the aphrodisiac aliments of which the two actors have made use.

The bed, simple in form, appears to be of bronze. There are several similar ones in the museum of Naples. They were found at Herculaneum and Pompeii.

Under the bed may be observed a stool.

SPINTHRIA

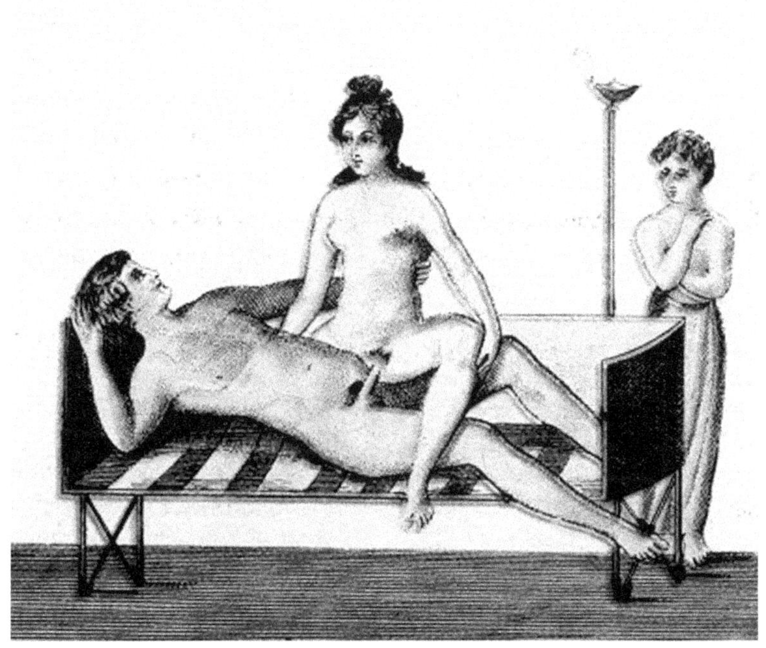

Plate XLVIII.

A YOUNG and beautiful married couple are amorously toying on a small bed. A lighted lamp shows that the scene takes place at night-time. As in the previous picture, the young man is carelessly stretched on his back, while his obliging companion, seated astraddle over him, is left to perform the principal part. In the background may be seen the cubicular slave, who is attentively watching the voluptuous pastime, and seems to be even looking on it with a lustful eye--

Masturbabantur phrygii post ostia servi,
Hectoreo quoties sederat uxor equo.

A circumstance which recalls the lines of Martial, already quoted.

This fresco is not without merit as regards its execution. The woman appears strong and well-formed; her fair hair falls over her shoulders in wavy curls. The man is beardless, but his stature is tall, and everything about him denotes a youth full of vigour and fire.

The bed, a very inconvenient one for such sports, is formed of a variegated cloth, of which the elasticity is not sufficiently seen. The curved head-board would indicate rather a kind of canopy than a bed. The whole is supported by four legs, too slender to resist long if they were not made of iron, a custom which has been perpetuated down to our own day in the south of Italy. It is, nevertheless, possible that this piece of furniture, so simple in appearance, was composed of a substance more precious than gold, for at the period of the decline, to which this painting belongs, luxury was carried to such a degree among the Romans, that it surpassed even the most marvellous stories of Eastern poets.

The Roman ladies attached great value to fair hair, though Nature had given them such beautiful black hair. It was indeed their habitual custom to have their heads shaved, and to cover them with light hair, which the young girls of Germany or Gaul sold them at fabulously high prices, Cosmetics of every kind were scattered over their toilet-tables; and we learn that Poppea, the wife of Nero, invented a pomade which received the name of poppeanum.

The same Poppea took baths of asses' milk to preserve her complexion; and Pliny informs us that she had five hundred asses milked daily for this purpose.

Every part of the known world at that time contributed to subserve the reckless and mad luxury of the Romans. India sent them fine pearl necklaces, valued at several millions of sistertii; [1] Arabia, her sweetest perfumes; Alexandria, Tyre, and Asia Minor, precious stuffs worked with gold and silk; Sidon, its metal or glass mirrors. Other countries sent to

---

[1] About six sistertii would make an English shilling.

Rome purple, gold, silver, bronze, all the productions both of art and nature, the choicest wines, and the rarest animals. [1] Under the later Scipio, men of high authority at Rome were seen wasting their substance with favourites, others with courtezans, or in concerts and costly feasts, having contracted, during the Persian war, the Greek tastes; and this disorder grew into a madness among the youths. [2]

M. Roux-Ferrand, collecting his materials from Martial, Pliny, Petronius, Seneca, Horace, Vitruvius, &c., has given, in his excellent work on the Progress of Civilization, a very fine description of those sumptuous repasts at which Roman luxury displayed all its pomp. We quote the following passage:--

"Bronze lamps, supported by candelabra, shed forth a glowing light the table, made of citrus-wood more precious than gold, rests on legs of ivory; it is covered with a surface of massive silver, of five hundred pounds weight, adorned with sculptures and designs. The tricliniar beds are of bronze, enriched with ornaments of pure gold and tortoise-shell; the woollen mattresses of the Gauls are stained with purple, and the costly cushions are covered with woven and silk-broidered coverlets, wrought at Babylon, and costing as much as four millions of sestertii (that is, about 630,000). The pavement, of mosaic, represents remnants of repasts, as if they had fallen naturally to the ground. The triclinium would hold a table with sixty couches; it was only intended for the summer, every season having its special utensils and slaves.

While awaiting the arrival of the master of the house, some young girls come in singing, and sprinkle on the pavement sawdust dyed in saffron and mixed with a brilliant powder. The table-cloth is a kind of incombustible flax, which is whitened by throwing it in the fire.

Young cup-bearers, natives of Asia, pour out all around perfumed wines cooled in snow; the cups are of gold, set with precious stones. During the repast, the guests, in order to refresh themselves, change their robes, and young girls, half-recumbent at their feet, beat the air and drive away the flies with fans of peacock's feathers, &c."

---

[1] Mazois, Bœttiger, Meiners (quoting Livy), &c, &c.
[2] POLYBIUS, ROUX-FERRAND, History of the Progress of Civilization.

APOLLO AND A NYMPH

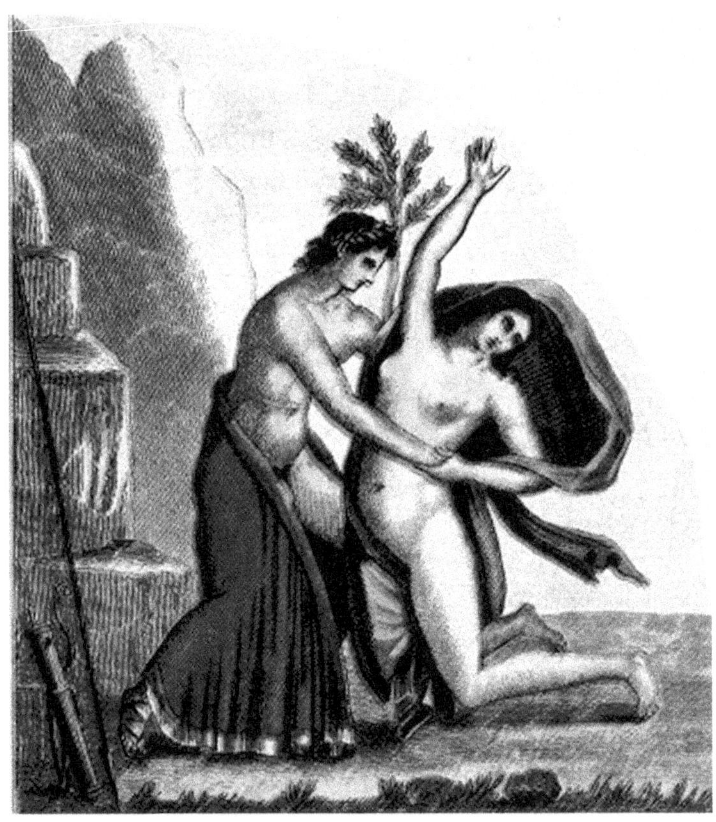

Plate XLIX.

IT is easy to recognise Apollo in the principal personage of this painting; but it would be difficult to assign a name to the young woman whom he is preparing to enjoy. It cannot be Daphne, for the god already wears a crown of laurel. Moreover, the mythologists have attributed to him such a number of mistresses, that it is impossible to ascertain whether the painter intended here to represent Coron is the mother of Æsculapius, Clymenes the daughter of the Ocean and the mother of Phaethon, Clytie, Leucothea, or some other.

Near Apollo we perceive a bow and arrows with a javelin: the scene is laid in a desert place.

The drawing of this fresco is, on the whole, bad; the limbs of the god's fair companion are perfectly gigantic, and the faces also are utterly devoid of expression. Nevertheless, the brightness of the colouring constitutes it one of the most remarkable paintings recently discovered at Pompeii.

AENEAS AND DIDO

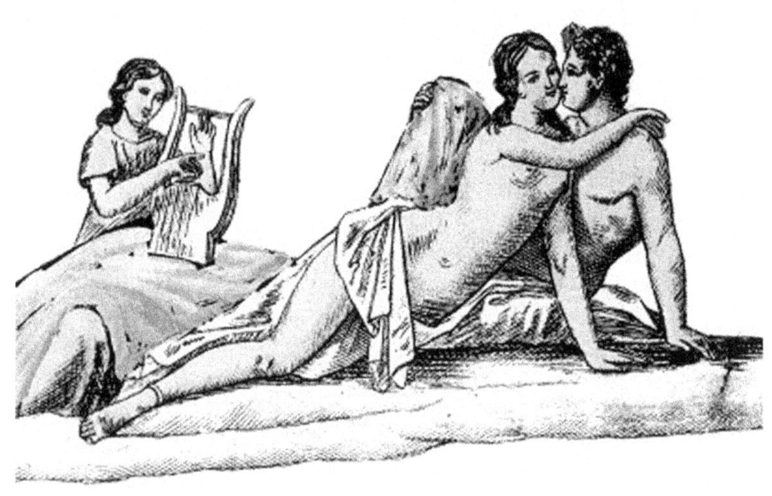

Plate L.

THIS fresco was one of the earlier discoveries, and was published by the Academicians of Herculaneum, and by Sylvain Maréchal, who considered the subject to represent Bacchus and Ariadne. They give as a reason for this interpretation the crown of leaves which may be observed, though not without some difficulty, on the head of the supposed Bacchus, as if it were not notorious that in erotic subjects the ancients usually represented their actors crowned with flowers and leaves.[1] The third person seen in the background seems to us triumphantly to refute the

---

[1] The Greeks and Romans, in their pleasure parties, crowned each other with the flowers which the season produced, especially with roses, to temper or dissipate the fumes of wine. They were first fastened to a linen or flaxen fillet, with which they bound their foreheads to avoid headache, the general consequence of drunkenness. A crown, interwoven with roses, violets, and ivy, was held to be the most salutary remedy against the heat of wine."-(J. B. LEVEE, in Plauto.)

assertion, seeing that Bacchus surprised Ariadne alone in a desert island. We look upon the following explanation as a more probable one:--

Dido has been informed that Æneas intends to fly; she implores him to give up this fatal project; and calls to her aid, in order to retain the hero, all the resources of love and beauty, which her sister Anna heightens, by the melody of her notes, the seductive illusion of this love-scene:--

Base and ungrateful, could you hope to fly,
And, undiscover'd, 'scape a lover's eye?
Nor could my kindness your compassion move,
Nor plighted vows, nor dearer bonds of love?
Or is the death of a despairing queen
Not worth preventing, though too well foreseen?" [1]

However the case may be, and if we take this to be merely a domestic scene, the third personage may be supposed to be a female musician, citharistria, placed at the door of the bed-chamber, and singing the Epithalamium.

---

[1] ÆN. iv. (Dryden's Translation).

SPINTHRIA

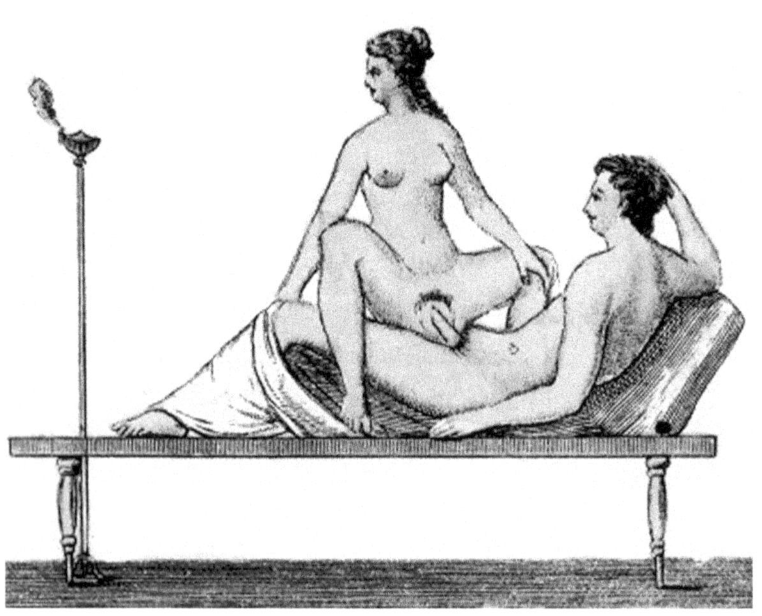

Plate LI.

ON a bed, of a shape equally simple and elegant, two young lovers are abandoning themselves to an amorous combat. The lamp which is flickering near them sufficiently shows that the painter has rashly betrayed one of those mysteries that have so much charm in the shades of night. When the importunate troop of cares that vex the day begin to rest, pleasure awakes, and the pale glimmer of a lamp often lights up scenes of happiness and intoxication in the alcove of an unfortunate man.

In this painting, of which the style is tolerably good, it may be remarked that both the actors are turning their heads in the same direction, and it is easy to perceive in their looks an expression of surprise and fear: it may be guessed that an untimely witness is approaching to interrupt them. [1] This circumstance recalls to mind the lines in which Horace paints, the happiness and tranquillity he enjoyed in the country:--

"No terrors rise to interrupt my joys,
No jealous husband, nor the fearful noise
Of bursting doors, nor the loud hideous yelling
Of barking dogs, that shakes the matron's dwelling.
When the pale wanton leaps from off her bed,
The conscious chamber-maid screams out her dread
Of horrid tortures; loudly cries the wife,
'My jointure's lost!'--I tremble for my life
Unbutton'd, without shoes, I speed away,
Lest in my person, purse, or fame, I pay,"

Horace, Sat., Bk. I, § 2 (transl. of the Rev. Philip Francis).

If the woman whom we see on this fresco is, in accordance with the painter's idea, a courtezan, we must not be surprised at the expression of fear which she manifests; for, then as now, these unfortunate women were not only subjected to the most rigorous scrutiny in their own houses, but were also a butt for the coarsest pleasantries of the young libertines who scoured the streets during the night, or went in the daytime to the temple of Venus, to amuse themselves at the expense of the courtezans, by smearing with soot the faces of those who did not please them. It is this custom to which Adelphasia alludes in the Carthaginian of Plautus:--

"I could wish, sister, you were less foolish: do you flatter yourself you are beautiful because your face has not been smeared with soot?"

The Romans made a distinction between courtezans (lenæ) and prostitutes (meretrices). The former made it a rule not to lie with any married man, and to remain faithful to the one who kept them as long as the agreement stipulated between them lasted; and it is to be noted that, for the most

----

[1] Fausta, the infamous sister of the famous Lucullus, had espoused Milo, whom the murder of Clodius and the speech of Cicero have rendered celebrated. Sallust, the historian, was the lover, or rather one of the lovers, of this woman. Milo, having surprised them in the very act, had a hundred stripes administered to Sallust, and did not let him till he had extracted from him a large sum of money.

part, this agreement was a written one. The law interposed in these kinds of contracts, and severely punished any courtezan who had concluded the same bargain with two lovers.

"Contrary to the decree of the law, you have received money from several." [1]

"Diabolus, the son of Glaucus, has given in free gift to Cleeretes twenty mines of silver, in order that Philenia [his daughter, a courtezan] may pass with him. and with no one else soever, her days and nights during this year." [2]

The courtezans only traded in their charms during the night, while the prostitutes remained at their doors, both day and night, to attract passers-by.

Both courtezans and prostitutes were compelled to have their names scribed by the ædiles; they could only belong to the class of freed men, or to that of women free by birth who were neither the widows, daughters, or granddaughters of Roman knights. Their dress differed from at of Roman ladies; they were clad in a short tunic, and a toga nearly similar to that of the male sex. They were not allowed to wear either gold or precious stones in public; and when they desired to deck themselves, one of their slaves carried their ornaments to the place they were going to, where they put them on and took them off before leaving. They mostly chose for themselves patrons or patronesses on whom they entirely depended. Those who belonged to slave-dealers paid a part of their earnings to their master, who kept a register, which he submitted to the inspection of the ædiles. Caligula was the first to impose the payment of a tax on them.

The courtezans, kept in this state of bondage through the influence of the Roman ladies, who did not blush at being jealous of them, took a brilliant revenge during the reign of the infamous Heliogabalus. This mad youth as even bold enough to enrol himself among them, and the example found numerous imitators of both sexes. [3]

---

[1] Truculentus, Act iv. sc. 2.

[2] PLAUTUS, Asinarius, Act iv. sc. 1.

[3] SUETONIUS, passim, PETRONIUS, cap. xl. TACITUS, Annal. TURNEL, Advers., p. 103 xvi. 19. C. LAURENT, de Adult. et Meret. cap. ii. BRISSON, Antiq. celest. FERRAR, de

SPINTHRIA

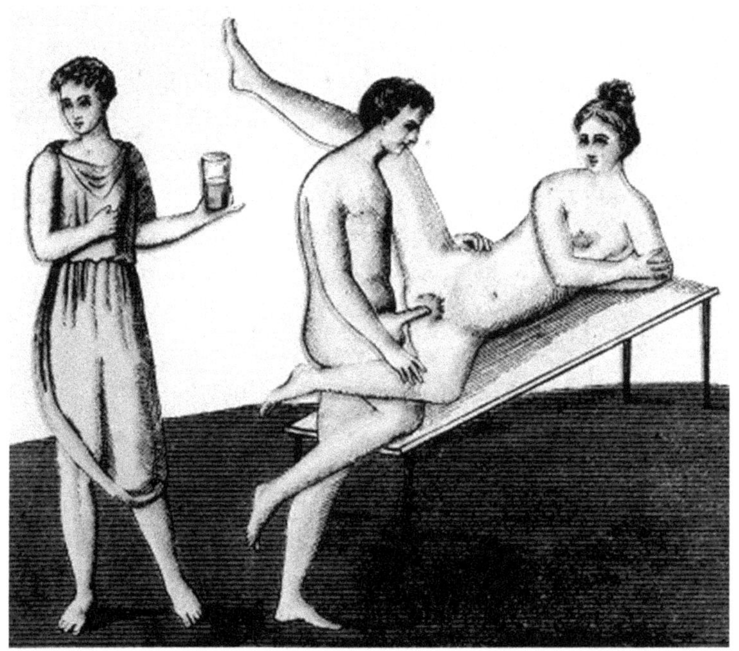

Plate LII.

THIS erotic scene is remarkable for the presence of the cubicular slave, a beautiful youth, who brings to the married pair a drinking-vessel, probably containing a comforting liquor, [1] turning his head

---

Re Vestiar, lib. I., cap. iii. and xxiii. J. B. LEVEE and l'abbe LEMOUNJER, Notes Arch. sur le Theatre des Latins, &c.

[1] In their parties of debauchery, the ancients took great delight in drinking water heated to a certain temperature, in which it is very probable they mixed some agreeable aphrodisiac to awaken sensuality. It is supposed also that they used hot water internally as a remedy tending to refresh them, and to restore to them part of the strength they had abused. SENEC., Wal. quæst., lib. III. p. 24; FREINSHERNI-

aside as he presents it to them, as if he blushed at their nakedness; with the same hand that holds the vessel he raises two fingers, a gesture which in our own day we should call the cuckold's sign, but which was not in ancient times a mark of insult or derision. It was simply a gesture to which was attributed the virtue of driving away witchcraft; and, as we said before, this superstition still exists in Italy. Possibly the young slave is desirous of keeping off the evil influences which might preside over the act of which he is a witness, and which will some day give him a new master.

The drawing of these figures is rather incorrect, and the expression cold.

NUS, de Calid. Potion, c. i. § 1 and 2"--(J. B. LEVEE, Notes, Arch. sur le Curculion de Plauti.)

SPINTHRIA

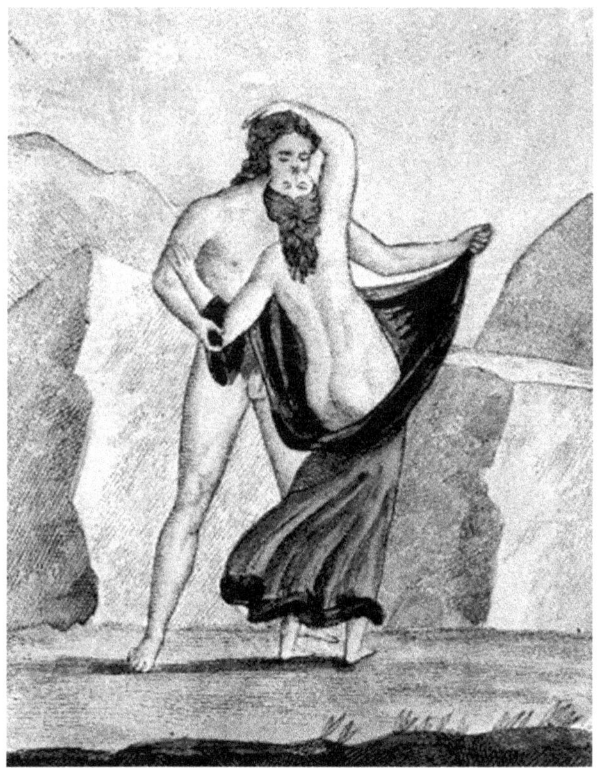

Plate LIII.

THE subject of this fresco is as ridiculous as the drawing is incorrect. How could a man, whom it is not possible to confound with a rural divinity, be thus in the open fields, in a complete state of nudity? or would he have dreamt, in such a place, of putting his mistress in the state, by removing her single garment? In this painting probability receives too great a shock, added to which the woman is twisting her neck in a horrible fashion to receive her lover's kisses.

These kind of obscene paintings (Spinthriæ) are frequently referred to by Latin authors. Here are two examples taken at random:--

The hand that first in naked colours traced
Groups of loose lovers on walls that once were chaste
And full exposed, broad burning on the light
The shapes and postures that abash the sight
Made artless minds in crime's refinements wise,
And flash'd enlightening vice on virgin eyes." [1]

"Looking up at a certain painting, in which was represented how Jove was said once to have sent a golden shower into the bosom of Danae." [2]

---

[1] PROPERTIUS, Elegies, Book i. 6 (translated by Elton).
[2] TERENCE, The Eunuch, act iii., sc. 5.

GROUP OF ANIMALS

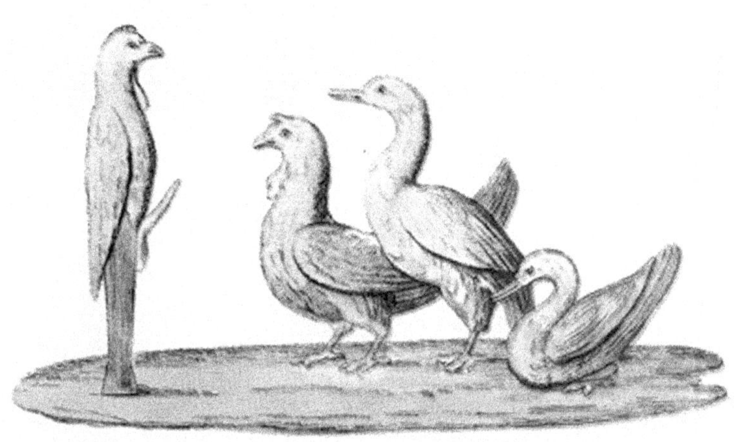

Plate LIV.

A PRIAPUS-HERMES, in the form of a cock, is receiving the worship of three birds--a turkey-cock, a goose, and a duck.

The artist's idea is not difficult to understand; it proceeds from the principle that everything in nature does homage to the generative power, animals as well as men, plants as well as animals.

The use of mosaics is too ancient to admit of our fixing its origin. The most received opinion is that it was transmitted to the Romans by the Greeks, who themselves received it from the Persians; but it was a long time making its way, for it was not until about the reign of Augustus that it became the fashion at Rome and began to spread in Italy. It soon became popular; every proprietor was desirous of having in his villa a saloon paved with mosaic; and it quickly passed from the saloon to the dining-room, and from the country to the town, till at last nothing was seen in the inside of the houses but mosaic pavement. It was introduced everywhere, into public buildings, and especially into temples. The Christians themselves adopted the use of it, and Italy possesses several churches in which fine work of this class is to be found. Thus, there may still be seen at Naples, in the cathedral itself, the chapel of St. Restituta, built, it is said, by Constantine the Great, entirely wainscoated with mosaic. The little town of Mont Real, near Palermo, also possesses some remarkable workmanship of this kind. The cathedral, a superb structure erected by Duke Rogero, is paved with mosaic representing gigantic heads of God the Father, Jesus Christ, the Virgin, the Saints, as well as subjects taken from the Holy Scriptures. It may be remarked in passing that in this same cathedral of Mont Real repose the remains of Saint Louis, King of France. They were placed there by Charles of Anjou, on the return of that unhappy Crusade, when the flower of the French army perished under the walls of Tunis.

We have purposely mentioned the mosaics of the chapel of Saint Restituta and the cathedral of Mont Real, because they are less known, though quite as remarkable as those at Rome and the other principal cities of Italy.

Antiquaries have not settled the entomology of the word mosaic. Some derive it from μοῦσον, polished, it being a kind of work much laboured and polished; others make it come from μοῦσα (muse), because it is a work worthy of the Muses or inspired by them; and lastly, there are some who suppose the origin of the word to be musivum, a delicate, ingenious work.

Mosaics were used, among the Romans, either to cover floors and the partitions of apartments or temples, or else to form pictures, furniture ornaments, or jewels.

At first the art simply consisted in fashioning little stones into cubic form, and arranging them on a surface of adhesive matter, while so co-ordinating the diverse colours as to form some design of arabesques, fruit, flowers, or any other object.

One instance will suffice to give an idea of the immense profusion of work of this sort among the Romans. It is well known that the sea-coast between Pozzoli, the ancient Puteolanum, and Mycene was formerly covered with superb dwellings, where the contemporaries of Cicero came to rest from town labours. These pompous abodes are now buried under the waters of the sea, which has recovered, on that side of the Mediterranean, the territory lost in other directions. Every day, for many years past, the tide washes on the shore fragments of mosaic of a hundred blended colours; and although the fishers of the place, and especially the children, carefully collect and sell them to strangers, the mine that furnishes them is still so rich, that the writer of this book collected in one day, and in the space of a single hour, more than he could carry away.

The second species of mosaic, that of pictures, furniture, and jewels, consisted in giving diverse forms to a quantity of precious marbles of different colours, so as to be able, on joining them together, to form a regular design, or else it consisted in colouring little stones or glass beads in order to form a description of painting out of them.

Glass beads were used in the more delicate work. When the artist had soldered them together, so combining them as to obtain an exact representation of the model laid before him, he delicately sawed the bundle formed by the union of the beads, and thus procured, in a single combination, a sufficient quantity of copies exactly like each other.

The mosaic forming the subject of this explanation is of the somewhat rare kind called monochromes. It is well executed and in good preservation.

PAN AND SYRINX

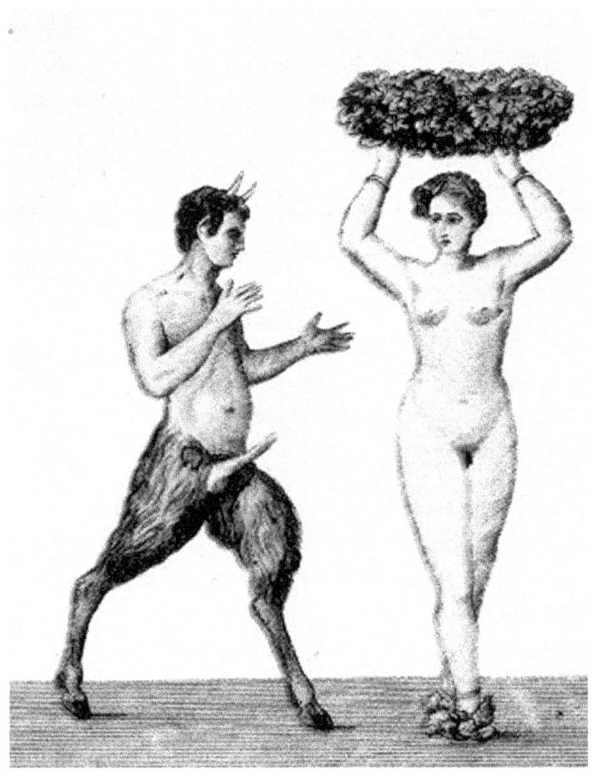

Plate LV.

THIS mosaic, in which is retraced the adventure of Pan and Syrinx, is unquestionably one of the finest pieces of the secret cabinet of the Museum of Naples,

We have already had occasion to say that several mythographers have very seriously called into question the reputation of chastity of the wife of Ulysses. According to their account, Penelope accorded her favours to every one of the numerous adorers who aspired to her hand and not knowing to whom to give the honour of an illegitimate son of which she was brought to bed, she named him Pan, from a Greek word, signifying all; thus attributing it conjointly to, the whole amorous community. Others suppose that Pan was the son of Penelope and Mercury. The messenger of the gods, they say, being unable to triumph over the chastity of the Queen of Ithaca, transformed himself into a he-goat, and thus attained his end; that is to say; Penelope granted to the animal what she had refused to the god. This was scarcely flattering to the latter; but the divinities of paganism were not very delicate on this point, and men received from them very bad examples. It is difficult indeed, to conceive that a religion so immodest could so long have resisted the progressive march of the philosophic spirits. It can only be explained by the reflection that the greater the corruption of morals became among the heathen, the more they strove to maintain a worship which not only excused the weakness of humanity but which sanctified the most infamous debauchery.

From the loves of Mercury and Penelope, then, was born a child, half-man and half-goat. This was Pan, who became the terror of the nymphs and shepherdesses. One day this lascivious god met the lovely daughter of the river Ladon, Syrinx, a nymph of Arcadia, and companion of Diana. She was peaceably coming down Mount Lyceum, unwitting the fate that awaited her; but at the approach of Pan, who manifested his desires in the most unequivocal manner, she began to fly rapidly. Her strength, however, was not equal to her virtue; she was nearly caught, and her defeat appeared certain when Diana, whose aid she invoked in this grave peril, did not abandon her, and the nymph was changed into a reed. The god, touched by his misfortune, stopped for a long time before the well-loved plant, whose foliage, caressed by the breeze, seemed to utter long groans. Pan, desirous of perpetuating the recollection of this sad adventure, and of rendering homage, at the same time, to the memory of the chaste nymph, formed, from several pieces of the reed, a rustic flute, to which he gave the name of Syrinx:

"Now while the lustful god, with speedy pace,
First thought to strain her in a strict embrace,
He fills his arms with reeds, new-rising on the place.
And while he sighs, his ill-success to find,
The tender canes were shaken by the wind,
And breathed a mournful air, unheard before,
That much surprising Pan, yet pleased him more.

Admiring this new music, 'Thou,' he said,
'Who canst not be the partner of my bed,
At least shalt be the comfort of my mind:
And often, often to my lips be join'd.'
He form'd the reeds, proportion'd as they are,
Unequal in their length, and wax'd with care,
They still retain the name of his ungrateful fair. [1]

---

[1] Metamorphoses, Book I. (translated by Dryden).

ETRUSCAN VASE

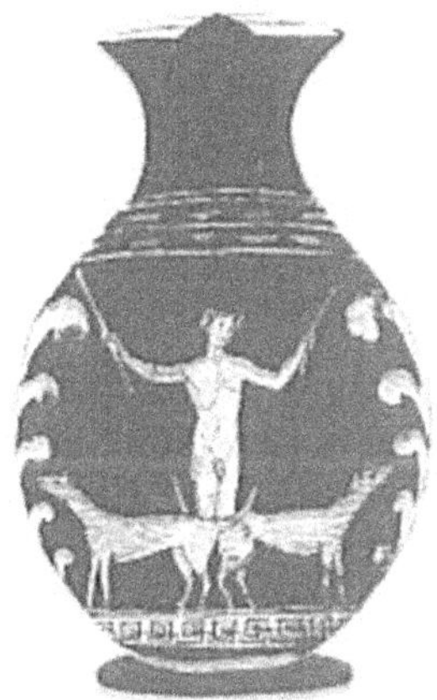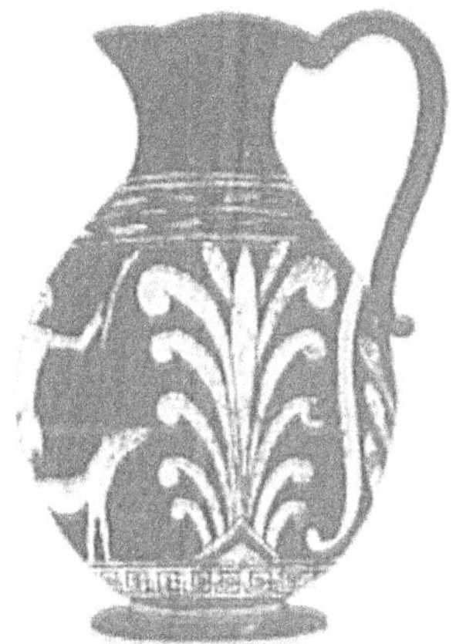

Plate LVI.

THIS is one of those far-famed vases, commonly called Etruscan, because the first were found in Etruria. Since then, a much greater number of them have been found in Graccia Magna, or Naples, in Greece proper, and in Sicily; and it has been admitted that they are of Greek and not Etruscan origin, so that it has been felt necessary to change their denomination. Among the divers names that have been proposed, the following have prevailed, or will at least assuredly prevail in the end: Grecian vases, those which belong to Greece proper; Italo-Grecian, those which come from Græcia Magna or Naples; and Siculo-Grecian, those which belong to Sicily. Finally, a fourth species of vase has been discovered, the fabrication of which may really be attributed to the ancient people of Etruria. The latter will retain the name of Etruscan vases; but, up to the present time, the collections of them are of little importance, and we shall not need to dwell on them.

Each of the three categories of Grecian vases is very easily recognized: it is enough to have made once or twice the comparison of one with the other two kinds. We may mention, in connection with this subject, that during our stay in Magna Græcia we often heard strangers express doubts as to the genuineness of Grecian vases offered to them, which doubts had no foundation whatever. There are at Naples several manufactories of pottery, imitative of the Etruscan and Grecian, from which charming table-services proceed, that would certainly have been improved upon in France if the introduction of foreign pottery were not prohibited there. But there is a wide difference between an imitation and a counterfeit, and the most casual inspection would enable any one, even a child, to distinguish the true vase from the false one. It is only necessary once to see them both together.

Grecian vases are found in the kingdom of Naples, in various parts but they are generally classed into Nola, Basilicate, and Apulian vases. Those of Nola are most prized, and unquestionably they are the finest, both for the elegance of their shape, and for the purity and splendour of their varnish.

The use of these vases was widely spread among the ancients; an immense quantity of them have been discovered, and the mine is still far from being exhausted. They were used for domestic purposes, for sacrifices, marriages, presents at divers periods of the year, and especially for funerals. When the body of the deceased person had been placed in the tomb, his relations and friends walked around it in succession, each carrying in his hand a little vase full of essence, with which he sprinkled the corpse, and which he afterwards placed in the tomb by the side of the dead. It was put in the folds of the mantle in which he was enveloped, on his arms, in his hands, and at his feet. And in the case of a rich person, the inside of the tomb was adorned with several large vases ornamented with beautiful figures, some filled with essences, and others bearing fruit or flowers. It is consequently in ancient tombs that the vases which form part of our collections are daily brought to light. In this respect those of Nola have another great advantage over the vases of Apulia and the Basilicate: they can mostly be removed without breakage, a very rare circumstance as regards those of the other localities, and which is thus accounted for. The custom of the inhabitants of Campania, and of Nola in particular, was to cover their tombs by means of two stones forming an angular roofing. This causes a greater strength of resistance to the spade of the excavator, who is promptly made aware of their presence, and takes the necessary precautions to draw them out in a good state of preservation. But this is not the case in the other provinces, where the tombs are sometimes entirely exposed, and sometimes covered merely by a flat stone. In the former case, the spade plunges into the bottom of the tomb and breaks everything it encounters there; in the latter, chips of the stone lid itself fall into the monument and injure the objects contained in it. The manufacture of this pottery among the ancients had, like the other arts, its childhood, maturity, and decline. The earliest vases are especially recognisable by their originality of shape and by the coarseness of the figures. Those of the decline generally have more pretentions and less elegant shapes than the vases of the best period. The figures in them are often loaded with dull whites.

We will now say a few words respecting the vases of the best period.

Only two colours appear in them: that of the original substance, reddish and clayey, and deep black. The Sicilian vases (Siculo-Grecian) mostly bear black figures on a reddish ground. The Italo-Grecian, on the other hand, usually have reddish figures on a black ground. This is not a rule without exception, for both kinds are to be found in both localities; but, in all cases, black is the only colour which the workman has super-added, red being that of the original substance. It was only, as we have already said, in the period of the decline that white was added.

Some vases are entirely black, or entirely reddish, without figures, or with nothing but a few arabesques, garlands, or fillets, and it is needless to add that these are the least prized. Amongst the vases with figures, most of the subjects represent initiations into different mysteries, games and wrestling, but it may be remarked that it is rather the rarity of the subject than the finish of the figures that tends to raise the price of these antiquities.

These vases are very varied in form, and many of them possess an elegance which renders them worthy to be used by our own artists as models, Each of the shapes is called at Naples by a particular name, derived from its resemblance to some modern object. The bell vase (campana) is that of which the opening, greatly extended, is wider than the body. See Plates LVIII. and LIX.

The Langelle vase, a graceful shape with two handles, for which see Plate LX.

The Nasiterne vase (see the Plate at the commencement of this chapter). The opening is divided into three compartments, and has the form of a trefoil. These vases have only one handle, The Cattino, a diminutive of catto, a bucket to draw water, when there is, over the opening itself, a handle in the shape of an arch. The balsaminæ, or lachrymatories, little vases with one handle, and with narrow necks, and body more or less protuberant. They are called Balsaminæ, because balms or perfumes were put in them, and lachrymatories, because the liquor comes out drop by drop, like the tears that fall from our eyes.

The lamp-vase, which assumes the shape of a small antique lamp.

Rhyton, having the shape of a hem. Cups, salt-cellars, ink-horns, &c.

We will not pursue this nomenclature any further, and we will refer those who desire to understand it thoroughly to a pamphlet of Canon Jorio, keeper of the gallery of Grecian vases in the Naples Museum.

The Plate opposite the first page of this chapter is a Nasiterne vase from Nola. [1] It shows a youth, crowned with leaves, holding two sticks in his hands, and to all appearance beating a dog and bitch with them, who are in the act of copulation. It would be difficult to say whether the artist had any mysterious hidden meaning.

---

[1] Nola. in Campania Felix, about fifteen miles from Naples. It is said that at Nola that bells were first used by the Christians, and hence were called campanæ.

HERCULES AND THE STYMPHALIC BIRDS

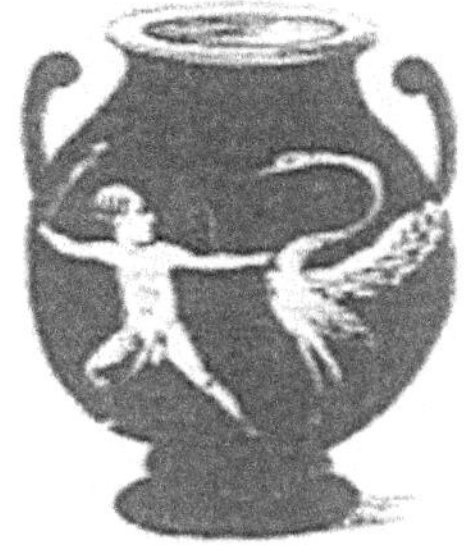 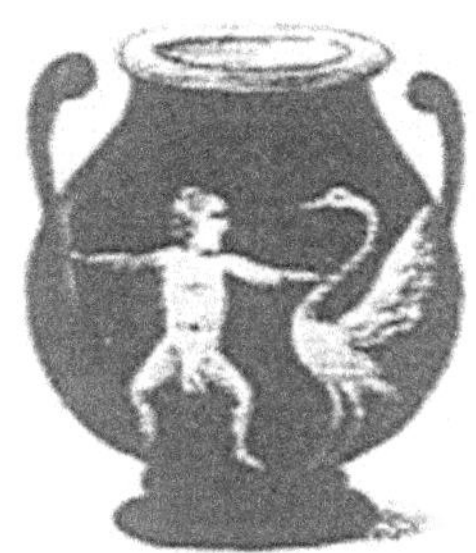

Plate LVII.

PAUSANIAS makes mention in his Arcadia of certain birds, which he believes to be natives of Arabia, of the size of cranes, and the appearance of storks. He adds that they sometimes came in large quantities, and established themselves in Arcadia, on the shores of Lake Stymphalus, whence they are called Stymphalides. Apollonius calls them πλοϊδας, that is to say, plungers or swimmers, a circumstance which proves that these birds, whatever fables may have been in vogue concerning them, belong to the family of imantopedes. It appears that these animals became more troublesome in the land of their adoption, and committed great havoc there. Those who delivered the country from them did it so great a service, that the imagination of poets seized hold of stories which gratitude had already exaggerated. This chase against birds, doubtless not very dangerous, became in their songs, and in the minds of the people, one of the labours of Hercules. It is said that, fleeing before this hero, they took shelter in an island of Pontus Axenus, [1] called Aretia, from Ἄρης, Mars, because the Amazons Otrera and Antiope had built a stone temple there in honour of the god; thenceforth the stymphalides were called birds of Mars. Apollonius Rhodius speaks of them in these terms:--

---

[1] Pontus Axenus, inhospitable sea, afterwards, when the coast was settled by Grecian colonies, called Pontus Euxinus, hospitable sea.

"The Mossynœcians next the country round
Possess, with mountains and with forests crown'd.
When these are past, an island bleak and bare
Lies full in view, there guide your ship with care,
And thence with care those noxious birds expel,
Which on the desert shore unnumber'd dwell.
Here form'd of solid stone, and seen from far,
Stands the rough temple of the god of war.
Two Amazonian queens, renown'd for arms,
Had raised the fane, when stunn'd with war's alarms."

A little further on he adds:--

"These nations past, with unremitting oar,
They reach, Aretias, thy sea-girt shore.
Then sunk the breezes with the closing day,
When down the sky descending they survey
A winged monster of enormous might,
Which toward the ship precipitates her flight.
Her wings she shook, and from her pinions flung
A dart-like quill, which on Oïleus hung." [1]

Timagnetes, a scholiast on Apollonius, writes on this subject: "These stymphalidian birds, whom Hercules drove away, had wings, beaks, and claws of iron." He sometimes calls them σιδηρόπτερους (iron-winged), sometimes σιδηρόνοχας (iron-clawed), and sometimes σιδηρόρυγχας (iron-beaked).

Pliny says in his Natural History:--"Opposite to Pharnacea is Chalceritis, to which the Greeks have given the name of Aria, and consecrated it to Mars; here, they say, there were birds that used to attack strangers with blows of their wings." [2]

---

[1] Argonautics, Book II. (Fawkes's Translation)

[2] Pliny's Natural History, Book VI.. chap. 12

BELL-SHAPED VASE

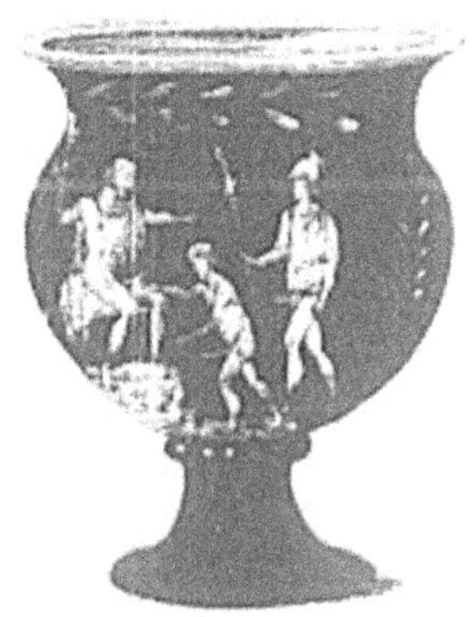 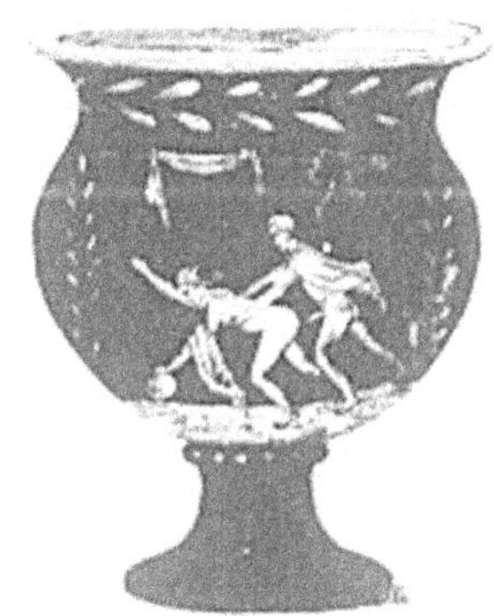

Plate LVIII.

THIS vase is of the kind which the Neapolitans call campana, on account of their shape, which has some resemblance to a bell.

On one side is represented a scene of the Dionysia or Bacchanalia. Three men are taking part in them, each furnished with preposterous phalluses. One of these personages is seated, and represents old Silenus: this is the hierophant, the president of the festival. To the spectator's right is a Bacchus covered with the chlamys, and with his head in a hairy casque. Between these two divinities may be seen a little old man, who draws near the hierophant, places one hand on his thigh, and prepares to worship the attributes of the god.

The other side represents a Bacchic game. A young woman is stooping to pick up the sphæra (a kind of ball) which she has dropped, but her awkwardness is equivalent to a defeat, and her adversary approaches her to exercise the rights of victory.

These two subjects are intermingled with foliage and with arabesques.

BELL-SHAPED VASE

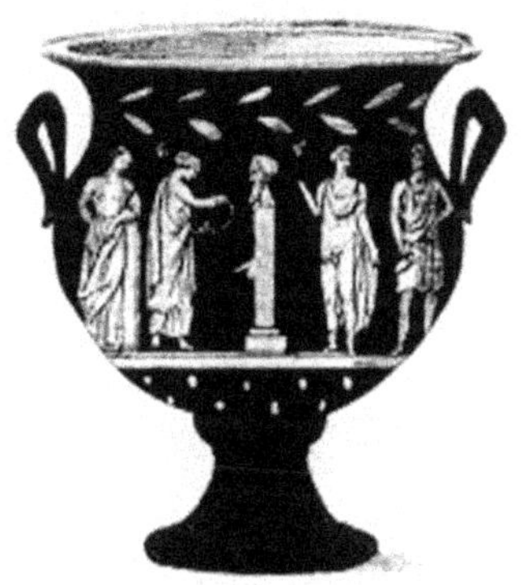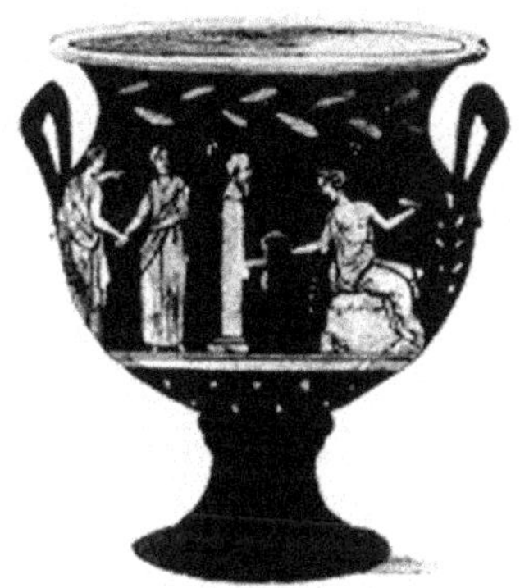

Plate LIX.

IN both sides of this campana may be seen male and female Bacchants offering crowns and garlands to Priapus. It is easy here to recognise the hierophant, the Bacchus, the priest entrusted with the ablutions, and the female Bacchants.

The figures are well executed. They bear peplos or chlamydes skilfully draped.

Of all the writers who have declaimed against the immodesty of the Pagan deities, few have done so with such force as Arnobius. Here is a rather curious fragment of his Treatise on the Images of the Gods (de Deorum Simulacris):--

"Why should I thus laugh at the false gods, at their horns; and ridiculous attributes, when I am well aware that they represent the habits of certain men and the features of certain infamous courtezans? Who does not know that the Athenians fashioned their Mercuries in imitation of the body of

Alcibiades? And who, on looking again into Posidippus, does not know that Praxiteles sculptured the Gnidian Venus after the courtezan Gratina, with whom the unfortunate sculptor was madly in love? But this Venus is not the only one whose face reproduces the features of a prostitute. Phryne herself, at the period when her beauty shone in all its splendour, and her youth was in all its freshness, served, it is said, as a model for the diverse figures of Venus, whether in the Greek cities or elsewhere where the worship of idols was admitted. The artists of that period strove in turn to surpass each other in reproducing the likeness of this courtezan in their statues of Venus, not in order that the goddess might become more august by it, but in order that Phryne might pass for the real Venus. The thing was carried so far that prostitutes received the sacrifices due to the immortal gods. We may cite the example of the celebrated Phidias, who, having made a statue of colossal size of Jupiter Olympius, graved on the finger of the god the name of a young and beautiful youth for whom he cherished an obscene passion . . . . .

"Thus, in bestowing a sex on the gods, if we invest them with the male organs of generation, we must expect to see them abandon themselves to acts which a chaste tongue could not even name. We must see them fired with passion like animals, wallow in the most degraded libertinism, and at last sink down into lassitude, weakened by excess of enjoyment; while, if we attribute the feminine sex to them, we must imagine the goddesses subject to the inconveniences of monthly terms, long and troublesome child-bearings, occasional abortions, and dreadful sufferings in their accouchement, &c."

LANGELLE VASE

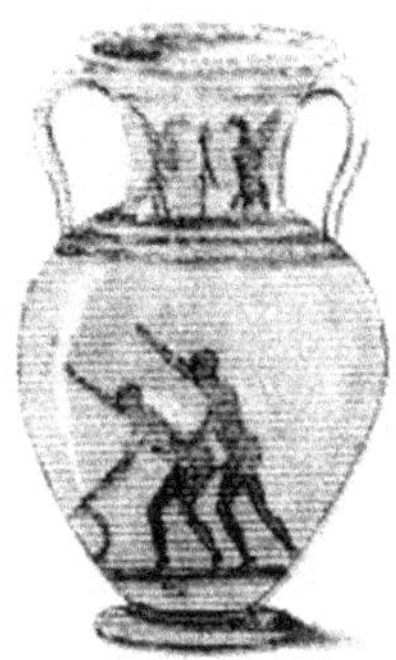 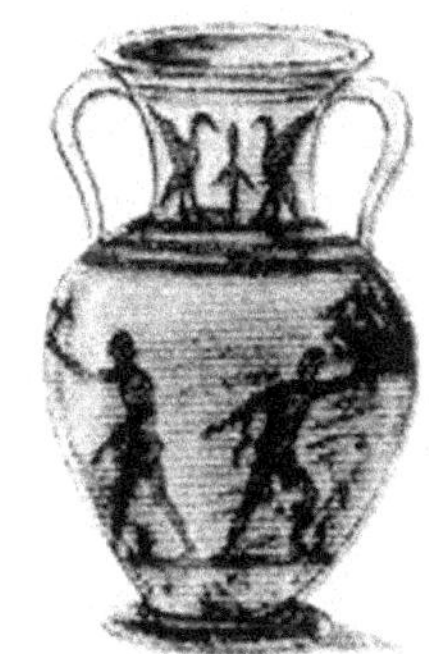

Plate LX.

THIS graceful langelle represents one of the most extraordinary of the gymnastic games known to the ancients. On one side may be seen two athletes armed with a kind of axe; on the other side the hoop has been substituted for the axe, and the conquered now undergoes the law of the conqueror. While the former stoops to pick up the disk he has clumsily dropt, the latter draws near him and prepares to enjoy his person: this was the law of the game. We may laugh at or despise the vanquished man, but we cannot envy the glory of the conqueror.

On each side of the neck of this vase is painted a thyrsus guarded by two cranes, coarsely drawn.

The number of Grecian vases with obscene figures is considerable, and some are to be found in most large collections. We do not, however, know of more than about half-a-dozen in the Naples Museum, independently of those we have just explained. The subjects they represent are so very much akin to the preceding, that it would have answered no purpose either to reproduce or to dwell upon them.